Kirtley Library
Columbia College
8th and Rogers
Columbia, MO. 65201

Managerial Stress

If, under stress, a man goes all to pieces,
he will probably be told to pull himself
together. It would be more effective to help
him identify the pieces and to understand why
they have come apart.

R Ruddock, *Six Approaches to the Person*, 1972,
p 94

Managerial Stress

edited by Dan Gowler and Karen Legge

A HALSTED PRESS BOOK

JOHN WILEY & SONS
New York – Toronto

First published in Great Britain
by Gower Press Limited, Epping, Essex. 1975

© Gower Press Limited 1975
Enid Mumford (Chapter 7)
David Weir (Chapter 10)

Published in the U.S.A. and Canada
by Halsted Press, a Division of
John Wiley & Sons, Inc. New York.

Library of Congress Cataloging
in Publication Data
Gowler, Dan.
    Managerial stress.

    "A Halsted Press book".
    Includes bibliography and index.
    1. Psychology, Industrial.
    2. Management. 3. Stress (Psychology)
 I. Legge, Karen, joint author.
II. Title.
HF5548.8.G67 1975   158.7   74-20107
ISBN 0-470-31985-2

Printed in Great Britain

Contents

Acknowledgements	ix
Notes on Contributors	x
Introduction *Stress, Constructs and Problems* Dan Gowler and Karen Legge	1
PART 1 INDIVIDUALS AND ROLES	19
1 *Stress, Motivation and Learning* J G Burgoyne	21
2 *Stress, Success and Legitimacy* Dan Gowler and Karen Legge	34
3 *Managerial Stress and the 'Cross of Relationships'* John Morris	52
4 *Stress and External Relationships: the 'Hidden Contract'* Dan Gowler and Karen Legge	70

PART 2
ROLES AND GROUPS   8

5
*Leadership Style in Stressful and Non-Stressful
Situations*
Philip W Yetton   8

6
Prerogatives, Participation and Managerial Stress
John Donaldson and Dan Gowler   1

7
*Stress, Uncertainty and Innovation: some examples
from the installation of large-scale computer systems*
Enid Mumford   1

8
Stress in the Management of Change
Allan Warmington   13

PART 3
ORGANIZATION AND CULTURE   15

9
Structure, Process and Stress
Tom Lupton   15

10
*Stress and the Manager in the Over-Controlled
Organization*
David Weir   16

11
Expectations, Chance and Identity-Stress
Eileen Fairhurst   17

12
Redundancy and Stress
Steve Wood   19

vi

Bibliography	210
Name Index	222
Subject Index	227

Illustrations

Figure 1:1 Activation scale. 26

1:2 Representation of the Yerkes-Dodson Law. 28

2:1 Stress: three interrelated perspectives. 35

3:1 The cross of relationships. 54

4:1 Aspects of the 'hidden contract'. 72

5:1 Alternative decision-making styles. 93

5:2 Managerial styles and levels of participation. 95

5:3 Interaction between stress and importance of acceptance. 97

9:1 The transfer of stress. 158

Acknowledgements

We would like to thank all our colleagues in MBS, including those whose contributions appear in these pages, for the interest and support they have given to this enterprise.

Our thanks go also to Penny Lloyd, Gower Press, whose encouragement and most helpful comments allowed us to transfer and cope with some of our anxieties.

Finally, we are most grateful to Mrs C M Brien whose patience and perseverance in typing the manuscript prevented the production of *Managerial Stress* from becoming too harrowing an experience.

Notes on Contributors

Dan Gowler (Editor) read Economics and Social Anthropology at Cambridge on a mature student state scholarship, having previously spent fifteen years in industry, most of this time employed by an oil company. He has spent the last eight years at the Manchester Business School where he is Senior Lecturer in Occupational Behaviour. His publications include books and articles on a range of topics, which include the supply and mobility of labour, wage payment systems and job satisfaction.

Karen Legge (Editor) is Lecturer in Organizational Behaviour at the Manchester Business School and Joint Editor of Personnel Review. She has carried out intensive field studies on the functioning of wage payment systems and labour turnover and is currently investigating the function of personnel management in a number of enterprises. Her publications include articles and essays in the general areas of labour economics and industrial sociology with particular reference to the operation of reward systems and internal labour markets.

John Burgoyne (Stress, Motivation and Learning) is Research Director and Management Teacher in the

Development Unit of Lancaster University. Prior to this he undertook research and lectured in management development at Manchester Business School. Dr. Burgoyne obtained a first degree in Psychology, a Masters degree in Occuptational Psychology and a Doctorate in Business Administration. He is Editor of *Management Education and Development*, the journal of the Association of Teachers of Management and author of a number of articles and co-author (with John Morris) of *Developing Resourceful Managers*, Institute of Personnel Management.

John Donaldson (Prerogatives, Participation and Managerial Stress) is a Lecturer in the Department of Management Science at Imperial College, University of London. He was formerly a Research Fellow at the Manchester Business School, and previously Research Assistant in the Economics Department of the University of Essex, followed by Tutor-Organiser of the Workers' Educational Association in south-west Lancashire. Mr. Donaldson has a Masters degree in philosophy, politics and economics and a Diploma in economics and political science from Oxford University. He carries out research and consultancy work in various industries and has written an MBS Occasional Paper on *The Paradox of Incomes Policy*.

Eileen Fairhurst (Expectations, Chance and Identity - Stress) is Research Associate in the Geigy Unit for the Study of Ageing, Department of Geriatric Medicine at the University of Manchester. Formerly she was a Research Associate at Manchester Business School, following a period in Canada as a Teaching Assistant and Research Assistant in the Department of Sociology, Carleton University.

Tom Lupton (Structure, Process and Culture) is Deputy Director and Professor of Organizational Behaviour at Manchester Business School. Previous posts include that of Head of the Department of Industrial Administration at Birmingham C.A.T. (now Aston University) and Montague Burton Professor of Industrial Relations at the University of Leeds.

Professor Lupton is Editor of the *Journal of Management Studies*, and has written several books including *Job and Pay Comparisons*, (Gower Press, 1973) co-authored by Angela Bowey. He is also Director of the Pirelli General Cable Works Ltd. and consultant to several companies.

John Morris (Managerial Stress and the Cross of Relationships) is Professor of Management Development at the Manchester Business School. Prior to this he worked in the Department of Psychology at the University of Manchester. Professor Morris holds a Bachelor of Science degree in Economics, a Masters degree in Business Administration as well as a doctorate. He is a part-time consultant to many large companies and works with NEDO and CNAA in management education and development. Professor Morris has written many articles and contributions to books in the fields of management development and social and development psychology and has co-authored two books, *Developments in Learning*, Staples Press (with E A Lunzer) and *Developing Resourceful Managers* Institute of Personnel Management, (with John Burgoyne).

Enid Mumford (Stress, Uncertainty and Innovation: Some Examples from the Installation of Large-Scale Computer Systems) is a Reader in Industrial Sociology and Director of the Computer and Work Design Research Unit at Manchester Business School. Prior to this she gained experience in personnel and production management and became a Research Associate at the University of Michigan, followed by the post of Research Lecturer at the University of Liverpool. Mrs Mumford holds a Masters degree, and is a Fellow of the Institute of Personnel Management. She is Joint-Editor of *Personnel Review* and author of several books and numerous articles.

Allan Warmington (Stress in the Management of Change) is Senior Research Fellow at Manchester Business School. He is also an external research consultant with a group of managers involved in a change programme, and is involved in teaching and research on problems of organizational change. Previously Mr Warmington was Senior Research Fellow at the University of Manchester Institute of Science and Technology, following posts with John Laing Research and Development Limited and the London School of Economics and Political Science. Mr Warmington obtained a Bachelor of Arts degree from Bristol University and is the author of several books and articles.

David Weir (Stress and the Manager in the Over-Controlled Organization) is Professor of Organizational Behaviour at Glasgow University. He was until recently Senior Lecturer at Manchester Business School. He started lecturing in the Extra Mural Department at Leeds University, moving to the Sociology Department at Hull University, and then Manchester University. Mr Weir holds a Bachelor of Arts degree and a Diploma in Public and Social Administration from Oxford University. He is on the Executive Committee of the British Sociological Association and has edited three books on social problems and the sociology of modern Britain, and is one of the authors of *Computer-guide III*, Programs for Social Scientists, National Computing Centre, 1972. He is currently working on a book on organizational crime and industrial deviance.

Steve Wood (Redundancy and Stress) is a Lecturer in the Department of Industrial Relations at the London School of Economics and Political Science. Prior to this he was a Research Associate at the Manchester Business School, involved in an SSRC comparative, industry-wide study of industrial relations. He graduated in Behavioural Science from Aston University and joined the doctoral programme at Manchester Business School. His Ph.D thesis was concerned with redundancy and involved intensive field work in three major firms at all levels of the organization.

Philip W Yetton (Leadership Style in Stressful and Non-Stressful Situations) is Senior Research Fellow at Manchester Business School where he is responsible for the teaching and research into managerial social-psychology. He holds a Bachelor of Arts degree, a Masters degree in Industrial Administration, as well as a doctorate. Dr. Yetton is a consultant in managerial psychology and is co-author of *Leadership and Decision-Making*, University of Pittsburgh Press, 1973 (with V.H. Vroom).

Introduction

Stress, Constructs and Problems

Dan Gowler and Karen Legge

In the introductory paragraph to his thoughtful and informative essay on the relationship between social stress and disease, Mechanic observes that

> 'Although the use of the term "stress" has not always achieved great clarity, the study of "stress" has brought together research findings from many different disciplines and points of view and has helped illuminate our understanding of human adaption'(1)

These comments, with their emphasis on the variety of approaches to the question of 'stress', provide an apt point of departure for the twelve essays which comprise this book. For each of the authors has taken a different line on the problem and illustrate Mechanic's observations on the range of disciplines, research and opinion involved as well as on the vexed question of the definition of stress.

This is all very well and, as editors, we could well leave the matter there and suggest that readers draw their own conclusions. However, commentators on this type of book often indicate that they believe it is the duty of the editor to find some common theme and/or derive some general conclusions from the various offerings. Consequently, we have made attempts to 'reduce the variety', and the outcome of these efforts is presented below.

First, some of our difficulties were dealt with because we asked contributors to consider the problem of *managerial* stress, thus narrowing the range and focus of their essays. Furthermore, we also requested contributors to relate their ideas on stress to everyday *managerial problems*, eg participation, innovation, performance and control. This request was not only aimed at the reduction of variety but also to ensure that 'stress' was not discussed *in vacuo*. We believe that it makes more sense to look at this phenomenon in context, which, as illustrated in several of the essays, has both theoretical and practical advantages.

Second, after receiving the various contributions, we decided to design the layout of the book along the lines indicated by the *theoretical constructs*, eg roles, structure and culture, used by the authors to define, illustrate and explain their ideas about stress and anxiety. These reflections led us to the notion that we might develop a 'model' of the book, based on generalizations about *the relationships between the two 'dimensions' discussed above*, ie practical managerial problems and theoretical constructs. Consequently, we present our own view* of the main themes of the various essays

---

*We emphasize 'our own view' since we must make it clear that the other contributors to the book have not been consulted on this point. Given this autocratic action, we accept complete responsibility for any of its failings.

through the 'model' illustrated in the accompanying figure.

The first theme represented is the level (column 10) at which the author concerned (column 2) has conducted his analysis. Furthermore, we have used this 'level of analysis' theme to determine the order of the chapters (column 1) which comprise the main contents of the book. Thus we moved from Chapter 1, where Burgoyne discusses stress in psychological terms at the level of the individual, to Chapters 2,3 and 4, where stress is dealt with in social psychological terms and the emphasis is on the individual in his or her social role(s). In Chapters 5,6,7 and 8, the contributors are still concerned with roles, but the emphasis shifts to the level of the group. The next two chapters, 9 and 10, take the analysis to the level of the organization, and here Lupton and Weir view stress in purely sociological terms. In the two final chapters, 11 and 12, Fairhurst and Wood deal with stress, or more precisely the use of the idea of stress, as a cultural phenomenon. Looked at this way, the order of the chapters follows the change in emphasis from the *individual* to *role* to *group* to *organization* to *culture*, and as such, the discussion of stress moves from the *psychological* and *social psychological* to the *sociological* frame of reference. However, we must make the point that the overall trend, represented in column 10, is a rather broad generalization since several of the contributors Gowler and Legge (Chapter 2) discuss stress at the level of the individual, role and organization, and thus use psychological, social psychological and sociological frames of reference.

These rather abstract notions about 'levels of analysis' and 'frames of reference' come into sharper focus when we consider them in relation to the two 'dimensions' mentioned above, ie theoretical constructs (column 3) and managerial problems (see horizontal axis spanning columns 4-9). However, we believe this sharper focus is best achieved by a discussion of how each contributor has actually

Figure 1 Constructs and problems

Chapter	Authors	THEORETICAL CONSTRUCTS	Style: Legitimacy Leadership Delegation Participation	Controls: Performance Information Evaluation	Change: Innovation Risk Uncertainty	Careers: Rewards Development Redundancy	Relationships: Interpersonal Relations (Internal and External)	Conflict: Mismatch Imbalance	Level of analysis
					(MANAGERIAL PROBLEMS)				
1	BURGOYNE	Level of activation	✓		✓				Individual
2	GOWLER and LEGGE	Role/Role set / Success criteria	✓	✓	✓				Role and role set
3	MORRIS	Cross of relationships	✓				✓	✓	
4	GOWLER and LEGGE	Role segregation					✓	✓	
5	YETTON	Contingency models	✓			✓	✓	✓	
6	DONALDSON and GOWLER	Alienation/ deprivation	✓	✓	✓			✓	Role/ role set/ and group
7	MUMFORD	Passive and active roles		✓	✓				
8	WARMINGTON	Change agent/ outsiders	✓			✓			
9	LUPTON	Structure / process			✓	✓	✓	✓	Organization
10	WEIR	Deviance	✓	✓	✓			✓	
11	FAIRHURST	Identity/ expectations/ labelling		✓	✓	✓		✓	Culture
12	WOOD	Ideology							

related stress, theoretical constructs and managerial problems. Limitations of space demand that these discussions are brief, but they do provide a guide to the contents of each chapter. Moreover, we use this guide as an opportunity to link one chapter to another and illustrate the idea that, despite differences of style and approach, the contributors do appear to agree on many points; we indicate some aspects of this consensus in the following summaries of each chapter.

In Chapter 1, Burgoyne makes the important point that the idea of stress confronts us with a difficult definitional problem. He comments that 'few, if any of us could offer a definition of stress that would meet with even a modest degree of general agreement. What is this phenomenon that we recognize but cannot describe?' It is interesting to note that this paradoxical question haunts the pages of this book, for every contributor has had to deal with it one way or another.

Burgoyne goes on to present a theory of stress, based on what he terms the *level of activation*. Briefly, he develops a 'rough formula' which indicates 'the extent to which we have experienced ourselves as more or less active and alert at different points of time...'. Significantly, this formula represents the idea that there is a multiplicative relationship between *uncertainty*, *importance of outcome* and *ability to influence outcome*. We use the word 'significantly' because the three variables which comprise Burgoyne's formula appear in one guise or another in almost all the chapters.

He also refers to 'the three ways in which stress can be coped with by the individual: *avoidance*, *defence mechanisms* and *learning*.' Again, these themes reappear in many of the contributions, and this is particularly true of 'avoidance'. Burgoyne introduces, also, some of the negative and stressful aspects of occupational roles and emphasizes the point that 'where practised, delegation usually *increases* stress.' We mention this because the question of delegation is considered in some detail by Donaldson and Gowler in Chapter 6.

We have discussed Burgoyne's contribution in relatively more detail than those which follow because we wish to establish a point of reference for some of the main themes of the book, while also using it as an example of how, in the figure, we have related theoretical constructs to managerial problems. Thus, the theoretical construct, level of activation, is recorded in column 3, while the managerial problems of delegation, outcome of the event, and uncertainty are scored under the general headings of 'style' (column 4), 'controls' (column 5) and 'change' (column 6), respectively.

In Chapter 2, Gowler and Legge develop their ideas about stress and anxiety through the theoretical constructs of *role*, *role set* and *success criteria* (column 3) and the managerial problems of legitimacy (style, column 4) performance and evaluation (controls, column 5) and uncertainty (change, column 6). In short they illustrate their approach to stress by the device of a model of the relationships between the *individual*, his *roles* and *organizational success criteria*. This model, which is also used to examine the role of the personnel specialist, emphasizes the importance of the influence of organizational success criteria in that they both define and evaluate roles. However, as Gowler and Legge also point out, for some managerial roles, eg the personnel specialist, the success criteria are either ambiguous, ill defined or even non-existent, which results in high levels of uncertainty, avoidance behaviours and so on. They also discuss organizational success criteria in relation to an issue which comes up elsewhere in the book - the question of *achievement*. They make the general point that individuals are likely to become anxious if, on the one hand, they feel they must achieve while, on the other, the success criteria which define and evaluate their achievement are either ambiguous or non-existent. Finally, Gowler and Legge suggest that individuals in these circumstances find great difficulty in establishing legitimate organizational roles, which may also be a source of stress and frustration.

It is interesting to note that Gowler and Legge, like Burgoyne, emphasize uncertainty and avoidance behaviours. Furthermore, their ideas about the need for and ability to achieve overlap with Burgoyne's views on the perceived importance of and ability to influence the outcome of an event.

In Chapter 3, Morris observes that 'managerial stress can be illuminated and to some extent relieved by considering the implication of some simple models of managerial relationships and managerial tasks.' He also makes the point that

> ...it seems useful to look for those **influences** that the manager has to deal with throughout the course of his working life. These flood in from four directions; from his seniors, and particularly his immediate boss, from his immediate juniors, from his working colleagues and from a variety of people outside the organization. These are not the only directions of information and influence, but they are most important.

Morris goes on to represent these 'four directions' by a model of the *'cross of relationships'* (column 3) and analyses stress in terms of the individual's ability to balance the often conflicting demands (column 9) stemming from these networks of interpersonal (column 8) and authority relationships (column 4).

It seems to us that there are two other general points of interest in his chapter. First, Morris is the most positive of all the contributors when considering how we might manage stress. Second, like Gowler and Legge, he emphasizes that stress is something to do with the pressures created by the failure to resolve a perceived imbalance or mismatch in one's circumstances.

In Chapter 4, Gowler and Legge deal in more detail with the stress created by external relationships and, as such, it may be viewed as a specific example of one section of Morris' cross of relationships. Briefly, they use the idea of *role segregation* (column 3) to examine the conflicts and tensions (column 9) that may exist in the relationship between husband and wife (column 8), particularly those resulting from mismatches between the demands of career (column 7) and family. (2)

In the four chapters which comprise Part 1 of this book, the emphasis has been on the individual and his role. Furthermore, these contributions tend to treat stress and anxiety in terms of the individual's ability to resolve the tensions aroused by some perceived mismatch or imbalance in his situation. Mechanic has called this the *stress adaption perspective* (3) and comments that

> It appears that it is useful to conceive of stress as characterizing a discrepancy between the demands impinging on a person - whether these demands be external or internal, whether challenges or goals - and the individual's potential responses to these demands. Generally, when discrepancies develop or are anticipated, they are associated with physiological changes, feelings of discomfort, and concern. The extent of physiological change and feelings of discomfort will depend on the importance of the situation or the extent of motivation, on the degree of discrepancy or failure anticipated or experienced, and on genetic and physiological factors.(4)

There are, however, other perspectives on stress, which are considered *en passant* in Part 1 and elaborated in the four chapters comprising Part 2. First, there is the perspective which considers stress in terms of group dynamics, and highlights the anxieties created by the use and abuse of power relations in social groups. This we term the *power-conflict perspective*.

This perspective is most clearly represented in Chapter 5, where Yetton discusses stress in the light of the degree of consensus and conflict (column 9) in work groups. Briefly, he develops a *contingency model* (column 3) which he uses to examine 'how managers both should, and do, vary their behaviour as a function of changes in the level of stress inherent in the problems which they face', where 'stress is treated as a situationally determined property and is measured in terms of the conflict between the manager and his subordinates.'.

Yetton also relates this model to questions of leadership and participation (column 4) and inter-personal relations (column 8). In the light of our earlier comments on general themes, it is interesting to note that Yetton pays particular attention to the question of *conflict avoidance* and speculates on why there should be so much. He goes on to suggest that: 'One possible explanation lies in the fact that socialization processes in both Britain and the US do not develop skills in solving interpersonal conflict! (5)

In Chapter 6, Donaldson and Gowler take up the argument about participation (column 4) and suggest that managerial stress may be generated by the *alienation* and *deprivation* (column 3) created by mis-understandings about power relations in contemporary work organizations. They also emphasize the point that conflicting values (column 9) about goals and performance (column 5) may exacerbate the anxiety and frustration aroused by inappropriate attempts to introduce participation in decision making, and suggest a more contingent approach to such innovations.

Chapters 7 and 8 take up the theme of change and innovation and discuss stress in the classic context of risk and uncertainty. However, these contributions focus upon specific managerial roles and offer useful insights into the difficulties faced by those who introduce and manage change in work organizations.

In the first of these two chapters, Mumford focuses on the problems associated with the installation of large scale computer systems. She comments that

> Computer innovation, because it is still comparatively new, yet developing rapidly, seems a particularly risky form of innovation. As risk situations can easily turn into stress situations, it is important to analyse the nature of the risks associated with the introduction of computer systems.

Mumford goes on to show how, in such situations of risk and uncertainty (column 6), the roles of those concerned may 'vary dramatically', and defines the type of role, eg *active* or *passive* (column 3), that might be adopted or thrust upon those concerned and, of course, the stress that is likely to result from 'playing' one or the other. Mumford also emphasizes the relationship between roles and the control of information and knowledge (column 5) and continues with an analysis of the conflicts of interest (column 9) and political behaviour as major sources of stress. She concludes with some observations on and suggestions about 'coping with the stress of innovation'.

In Chapter 8, Warmington describes 'the environment in which the management of a change programme is likely to be set up, and analyses the sources of stress which are inherent in the situation.' He also relates his analysis of this type of situation to the role of the *change agent* (6) (column 3) and discusses the particular difficulties associated with the change agent as an *outsider* (7) (column 3).

Warmington emphasizes, too, the anxiety aroused by the inability of the change agent to establish a legitimate role (column 4) which is often accentuated by risk and uncertainty (column 6), particularly that related to career expectations (column 7). For example, he comments that

> The people selected to be members of the change programme are likely to be young, successful managers from established positions, probably from a number of functions and disciplines, who are recognized by their superiors, and who perceive themselves as having considerable potential for advancement. These managers are removed from positions where the criteria for success are relatively clear, and where they have conformed to these criteria. They are transferred into a new role and a new situation where none of this applies, and where performance in previous roles appears irrelevant.

Apart from raising the very important issue of the relationship between *stress and transfers*, Warmington restates the point made by Gowler and Legge (Chapter 2) that the absence or ambiguity of the criteria for success is a source of dissonance and anxiety.

The final section of the book, Part 3, moves the debate to the level of the organization and culture. As we have commented above, Part 2 reflects the power-conflict perspective on stress but, in Part 3, two more perspectives emerge - the *structural* and the *labelling perspective*.

The structural perspective views stress in terms of the pattern of social relationships, ie social structure, in which individuals and groups are enmeshed. Put simply, in this view, stress is likely to be generated by frictions and changes in the pattern of social relationships, which disturb settled expectations, roles, controls, the distribution of power and so on.

The labelling perspective recognizes and highlights the fact that all social structures, particularly work organizations, may be viewed as systems of social control. Moreover, it emphasizes the point that social control rests on social definition, and that social definition requires categories or labels.

However, though labels may be seen as an aspect of structure, in that they help to define and regulate social relationships, they are also a cultural phenomenon, since they involve values, beliefs and symbols. As we discuss later, there are subtle and complex relationships between labelling and the arousal and reduction of stress, but suffice it to say here that these ideas introduce a novel and stimulating dimension to the debate.

In Chapter 9, Lupton examines stress as a property of *structure and process*, and on the concept of structure, observes that

> The idea of *structure*, as it is generally conceived, refers to a set of parts linked according to some principle or principles to form a persisting whole. When we speak of *social* structure, the parts referred to are social positions, not, we emphasize, individuals, but the positions they may occupy from time to time.

Further,

> The existence of social structure is inferred from observations of what is said and what is done. It is an abstract idea, since it does not include all that could possibly be observed in social relationships, activities, or events. The signs of structure are, of course, behaviour that recurs, exhibiting pattern and regularity.

On the question of process, he comments that

> The concept of *process* includes time. The observer interested in process notes what is happening; he is much more sensitive to the way that events and activities are related to other events and activities in time sequence. There may be and usually are regularities, also cycles of events, cumulative processes like self-fulfilling prophecies, virtuous and vicious circles, and so on. There may also be unexpected irregular con-

junctions of activities and events, ie as they appear both to the observer and the participants, which lead to new 'turns of events'.

Lupton goes on to relate the concepts of structure and process (column 3) to aspects of control (column 5) and to interpersonal and intergroup conflict (columns 8 and 9). He also uses two examples to illustrate the relationship between these ideas and what he terms the *transfer of stress*. It seems to us that this idea about the transfer of stress would repay further discussion and research, since it links the reduction and avoidance of anxiety with organizational change. Apart from its theoretical interest, this idea has practical implications for organizational development and design.

In Chapter 10, Weir makes the distinction between two different (and not necessarily related) ways in which we talk about stress; he comments:

> The expression is often applied to the effects of occupying a particular position in an organization. So we read of stress in the job of an airline pilot, or the stresses and strains of occupying a top managerial post. This is *individual* stress. Managers, of course, normally expect to occupy a position in which stress of this kind is one of the features. *Organizational* stress is a far more insidious phenomenon; it is the process by which a firm or institution becomes deformed, slowly and systematically, by the constant malfunctioning of some system.

Weir goes on to argue that one type of organizational stress is created and amplified by *overcontrol*. Briefly, he shows how social *deviance* (column 3) is aggravated and perpetuated by heavy-handed and inappropriate attempts to control (column 5) behaviours that are not fully understood. Like Lupton, he also shows how the stress and conflict (column 9) is transferred around the system, resulting in avoidance behaviours, insensitive forms of intervention (column 4) and so on.

As commented above, the remaining two chapters are examples of what we have termed the labelling perspective on stress. Thus, in Chapter 11, Fairhurst relates ideas about *expectations, identity* and *labelling* (column 3) to risk and uncertainty (column 6) promotion systems (column 7), and perceived mismatches (column 9) between expectations and action. Additionally, after having 'sketched out potentially stressful situations for managers', she focuses her attention on luck-labelling as a response to identity stress, and states: 'I want to suggest that one of the ways that managers may attempt to preserve their identity is to account for events in terms of luck'.

It seems to us that there are two general points that we should make here. First, Fairhurst draws attention to the fact that we use labels in an attempt to give meaning to and exercise control over ourselves and others. The form that these labels take obviously varies from culture to culture, thus 'luck' or 'being lucky' is emphasized in some societies and not in others. Second, she argues that, in our culture, we use the luck-label to help cope with certain types of stress. However, in doing this, she implies that our use of such terms as stress and anxiety may actually be such labels, fulfilling functions other than a description of an unpleasant emotional state.

This 'radical' approach to the idea of stress and its uses is more clearly stated in Chapter 12. In this contribution, Wood develops a critical approach to the conventional view that 'redundancy is a time of stress'. Further, using a wide range of shot and a broad spread of fire, he suggests that managerial *ideologies* (column 3) tend to explain and justify stress and its related problems at a purely psychological level. He also suggests that this not only encourages a form of cultural self-deceit, but actually masks fundamental problems created at the level of the organization and society. In passing, he also relates his analysis of redundancy (column 7) and stress to a number of managerial problems, eg flexibility and performance (column 5) and insecurity (column 6).

We must now make it quite clear that our model of the book, as illustrated in the figure, is a grossly oversimplified version of the views, theories and suggestions put forward by the contributors. We also wish to emphasize that we do not claim that this book covers all the known theories about stress, or that the theoretical constructs and managerial problems outlined in the figure are in any way comprehensive. However, we claim that the ideas presented have a general application and are not necessarily reserved for those in managerial posts. Thus, for example, shop floor workers suffer role conflict, insecurity, and have problems with their interpersonal relationships. In other words, they also experience stress and anxiety for reasons similar to those described above. Given these comments, we conclude with a review of our perceptions of the main themes of the book. It must be borne in mind that, while we distinguish five distinct themes, they are interrelated in a variety of ways - as indicated in the figure.

First, we have come to the conclusion that stress, whether treated at the level of the individual, group or organization, is related to the degree of coercion and control perceived to exist in the situation. Thus, 'overcontrol' may lead to deviance and stress, while 'undercontrol' may result in uncertainty and stress.

Second, stress is clearly associated with mismatch, imbalance and discontinuity. It is interesting to note here that it has been claimed that some of the longer-lived people in the world, the Abkhasians, are said to place a high value on balance and continuity, and thereby avoid the stresses associated with change and innovation. (8)

Third, stress appears to be related to hierarchy and power, in that the latter almost inevitably involves both conflict and coercion, particularly in cultures where personal achievement and competition are very highly regarded. It is also apparent that stress may be generated by intra - and inter-role conflict and the pattern of interpersonal relationships. This familiar type of stress is often the result of interpersonal and inter-group conflicts over the distribution of power, prestige and material rewards.

Fourth, stress appears to be the ever-present companion of the specialist, be he change agent, personnel manager or whatever. An explanatory hypothesis about the relationship between specialization and stress is put forward in two of the contributions (see Chapters 2 and 8) and suggests that specialists who have difficulty in establishing acceptable success criteria for their roles are likely to experience feelings of anxiety, frustration and failure.

Fifth, we have noticed that several of the contributors emphasize the fact that stress results in a variety of avoidance behaviours, defence mechanisms and so on. Furthermore, one contributor - Yetton - argues that, in our society, stressful conflict is likely to be resolved by authority or that its very existence may be denied. In either case, the conflict is avoided and/or transferred. These avoidance behaviours are interesting in themselves and certainly warrant further attention, but when the cultural prescription 'Thou shalt avoid' is juxtaposed with the equally important 'Thou shalt achieve', a considerable amount of tension is likely to be the result. The point here is that achievement generally requires cooperation (and entails conflict), which to all intents and purposes rules out most social avoidance behaviours. While it is easy to see how this 'tension' might itself be a source of stress, it might also be speculated that it is a 'dynamic tension' and, as such, provides one of the mainsprings of change and innovation in our society.

Finally, the definition of stress appears to remain a problem. Perhaps even more so after the challenging views expressed in Chapters 11 and 12.

However, our view of stress and its definition is similar to that taken by Nadel, who, after analysing the difficult and abstract concept of social structure, observes:

> Thus, paradoxically speaking, we profit not from having defined a social structure, but from trying to define it, not from having made the study but from making it.(9).

References

1 D Mechanic, *Medical Sociology, A Selective View*, Free Press of Glencoe, New York, 1968, p 294.

2 For a recent discussion of the relationship between family, work and leisure, see M Young and P Willmott, *The Symmetrical Family: A Study of Work and Leisure in the London Region*, Routledge and Kegan Paul, 1973.

3 D Mechanic, op cit, p 301.

4 ibid, p 301.

5 For a comparative discussion of child-rearing practices, see U Bronfenbrenner, *Two Worlds of Childhood: USA and USSR*, George Allen and Unwin, 1971.

6 See E M Rogers and F Floyd Shoemaker, *Communication of Innovations, A Cross Cultural Approach*, Free Press of Glencoe, New York, 1971, pp 228-48.

7 The importance of the role of the outsider in a community is shown, for example, in R Frankenburg, *Village on the Border*, Cohen and West, 1957.

8 S Benet, *Abkhasians, The Long-Living People of the Caucasus*, Holt, Rinehart and Winston, New York, 1974, pp 103-8.

9 S F Nadel, *The Theory of Social Structure*, Cohen and West, 1957, p 154.

PART 1
INDIVIDUALS
AND ROLES

1

Stress, Motivation and Learning

J G Burgoyne

THE PHENOMENON OF STRESS

Almost everybody has a clear idea of what they are talking about when they refer to personal stress, particularly their own. Furthermore, most of us seem to be referring to more or less the same thing when we discuss it; we rarely have the experience that others are using the word to label a completely different phenomenon. Yet few, if any of us, could offer a definition of stress that would meet with even a modest degree of general agreement. What is this phenomenon that we recognize but cannot describe?

If one asks people about *their* stress and, in particular, how they know it exists, two general kinds of thing are described. Firstly, there are experiences of mental discomfort, often accompanied by feelings of not being able to cope, that things are falling apart, that one is not in control of oneself and one's situation, or just a general unease that all is not well, without any particular cause being apparent. Secondly, there are the physiological manifestations of loss of appetite, sleeplessness, sweating and, maybe, ulcers or other physical illness, of various degrees.

The physical side of stress seems to be relatively well understood. Briefly, it is that the body reacts to prepare itself for violent activity, as in fight or flight, but that in our society such physical activity rarely follows, so the physical system is thrown out of balance with excess acid secreted in the stomach, adrenalin and fat in the blood, and so on. It is not so clear what process sets off these reactions, and how the psychological or experienced aspects of stress are to be explained. It seems highly likely that the two are closely related.

My aim here is to develop some ideas about the psychological nature of stress and to look at what this implies for individuals and organizations trying to cope with it. The basic premise is that stress is fundamentally a psychological phenomenon, with immediate and direct physiological manifestations. Just as a physiological disturbance is often accompanied by the experience of pain, so psychological disturbance can be accompanied by physical manifestations as well as an experience of discomfort. In fact, the association between stress and pain is very close.

The experience of pain discourages us from deciding to do things that are physiologically damaging to ourselves. Pain is therefore *functional*. It may well be that stress, or at least the discomforting experience of it, is also functional in signalling that we are doing something psychologically damaging to ourselves, and as a mechanism for discouraging us from continuing.

A THEORY OF STRESS

I suggest that people find different events, situations, activities involving and activating according to the rough formula: (1)

Activation = Uncertainty about the outcome of the event ✕ Importance of the outcome of the event ✕ Ability to influence the outcome of the event

The following points need to be made about the elements and relationships in this equation.

Activation

The formula assumes that people do vary from one point in time to another in their level of activation. Activation is regarded as a one-dimensional variable, so that for any person at a given time it is high, low or somewhere in between. There is a certain amount of evidence from physiological studies of the body and studies of electrical activity in the brain to suggest that the concept of activation makes a certain amount of sense. Perhaps equally important is the subjective evidence of experience. To the extent to which we have experienced ourselves as more or less active and alert at different points of time, we will find the concept of 'activation' useful.

Uncertainty

The uncertainty of the outcome is also presumed to be a one-dimensional variable. This variable, like 'importance' and 'ability to influence', is intended in the subjective or perceived sense, rather than in the external or objective sense. It is how uncertain the person *believes* the outcome to be, rather than the objective uncertainty, which is important. Typically, perceived uncertainty will approximate - through a process of learning - to objective or actual uncertainty. Finally, it is important to note that as a person develops his *skill* in coping with a certain class of situation he will increasingly be able to control outcomes and therefore reduce uncertainty. So long as he is aware of his increased skill this greater perceived certainty will enter the equation and reduce overall activation. This may well be the process we experience as our confidence at a new task grows.

Importance of Outcome

This again is a subjective variable, but in this case there may not even be an external or objective 'importance' which it is adjusted against. The term really begs the question: what outcomes are important? For our purposes, we have to assume that for different people different things are more important, but that for any one person some outcomes are more important than others. How individuals come to have these priorities and preferences is beyond the scope of this discussion.

Ability to Influence Outcome

This subjective variable does, in principle, have an external, objective counterpart; it is a question of fact whether a given person's choice of action in a given event influences the outcome of that event or not, and if so to what degree. An important point needs to be made to clarify this variable: it is the person's perception of his ability to *influence* the outcome, not *control* it, which is in question. Thus, the novice driver and experienced driver sitting in the driving seat of a car both have the same *influence* by **virtue** of the fact that they have access to the same controls. They are likely to differ in terms of *uncertainty of outcome* because the novice is likely to perceive himself as less skilled and thus - other things being equal - the novice will find the situation more activating.

The Multiplicative Relationship

Presenting the equation in a quasi-mathematical form

is not intended to imply that all the variables can
necessarily be precisely measured on a scale and that
they relate in a highly precise mathematical way.
However, the formula is intended to imply that the
three variables do function through some psychological
process to cause the level of activation, and that
the way in which the three variables combine to do
this is approximately multiplicative. An implication
of the multiplicative relationship rather than, say,
an additive one is, for example, that if any one of
the three variables is almost zero, then activation
will be minimal no matter how high the other two are.

SCALE OF ACTIVATION

The theory as so far described suggests that
uncertainty, importance and ability to influence
combine to determine a level of activation which can
be roughly defined as the level of psychological
energy that the given situation stimulates. This
scale of activation can be roughly divided into three
areas. At a very low level of activation, the person
will not be sufficiently activated to do anything in
the situation. If he does perform a task it is
because he is coerced into doing so by promise of
reward or threat of punishment, or, in other words,
the situation is redefined by having some more
important outcome made contingent on task performance.
As situations become more activating, they
intrinsically stimulate a level of activation which
makes the person active in that situation. As the
level of activation increases, the amount of psychological energy released to work on achieving
important outcomes also increases.

However, there is likely to be a maximum amount of
psychological energy that the system can constructively
use to work effectively in the situation. When the
released energy exceeds this amount, the excess will
'overflow' into the system with destructive consequences, and this is the condition that we call
stress with its manifestations in experience,

behaviour and physiological reaction. Here the
theory follows a mechanical analogy: up to a point
the more energy that one puts into, say, a gearbox,
the more that comes out. Beyond a certain point,
however, it cannot cope; the energy 'overflows' within
the machine, causing overheating and impairing even
the existing capacity to transmit energy. The
activation scale can therefore be drawn as in
Figure 1.1.

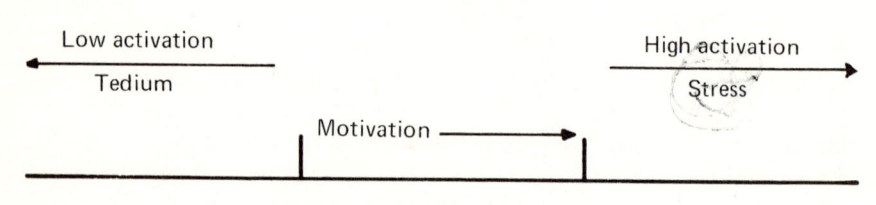

```
←———— Low activation ————                    ———— High activation ————→
         Tedium                                       Stress
                        |———— Motivation ————→|
```

Figure 1: 1 Activation scale

Before we look at the validity and usefulness of this
framework, one further development is useful. So far,
stress and activation have been considered in single
events and at single points in time. This is
obviously a simplification. In reality, everyone
is involved in many sets of activities, sometimes
pursuing several at once, sometimes switching fairly
rapidly from one to another. It is therefore useful
to think of people as having 'portfolios' of activities
which they are concerned with, and attending to these
in various combinations and sequences. Each of the
activities in the portfolio, as well as the new one
of managing the allocation of effort between the
demands of the activities comprising it, generates its
own level of activation. Over time, it seems that
people can tolerate some activities which generate
a high level of activation provided they are involved
in other less demanding activities as well. Thus,
stress is not just a matter of peak levels of

activation, but is associated with a high *average* level of activation over time, or the cumulative effect of a high level of activation over time. Alvin Toffler (2) has suggested the concept of the 'personal stability zone' as a way of coping with the stresses of modern life. This involves keeping an area of one's life fairly constant as a base from which to become involved in change in many other areas.

The Validity of the Theory

This framework is offered primarily in the hope that it will help the reader to make sense of, and cope with his experiences of stress in himself and others. Its main claim to validity is that others have found it useful in this way in the past. There are, however, some research conclusions that support parts of the theory:

Performance Peak

Yerkes and Dodson (3) showed that, for a learning task performed by mice under varying degrees of need state, performance increased up to a certain level of need, and decreased thereafter, and that the point at which the motivating force became dysfunctional came earlier for tasks of greater complexity. These findings have been well replicated by Hammes (4) and Broadhurst (5). In general, the results are as shown in Figure 1.2.

This result supports the theory in two ways. Firstly, it shows that an increase in the need state, which can be seen as equivalent to importance of outcome, is motivating up to a point but, beyond that, destructive in terms of performance. This is consistent with the theory. Secondly, it shows that with a more complex task, in which there is presumably less certainty about the outcome, the point of diminishing return is reached earlier. This is therefore consistent with the theory that importance of outcome and uncertainty of outcome increase activation which, in turn, leads to decreased effectiveness at a certain level.

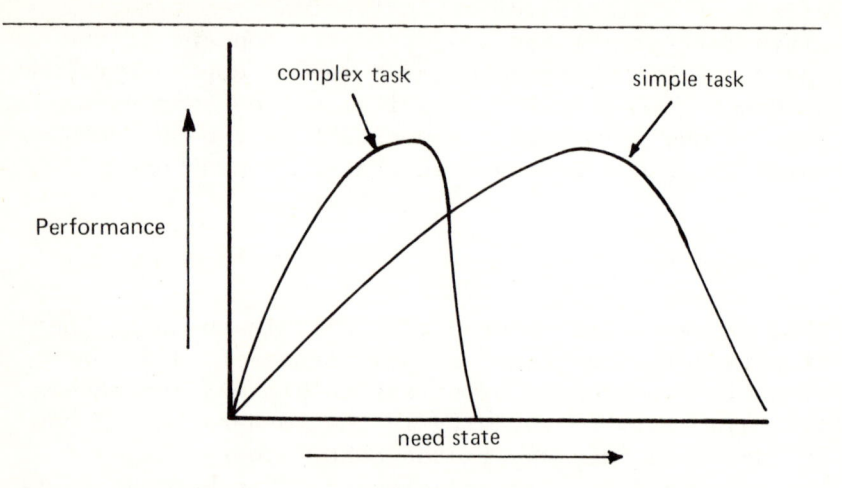

Figure 1: 2   Representation of the Yerkes-Dodson Law

Stress and the Ability to Influence Outcome

The relation between ability to influence outcomes and stress is clearly shown in Brady's classical experiment of the 'executive monkeys'(6). Two monkeys were placed in identical chairs where they *both* received mild electric shocks every 20 seconds unless one of the monkeys pressed a button in the intervening period. The other monkey had a button which was not wired to anything, and hence got exactly the same shocks as the other monkey, but without any influence on them. The monkey with influence over the shocks typically developed stomach ulcers in a relatively short period, while the other one remained ulcer-free.

COPING WITH STRESS

If there is any validity in the suggested framework for thinking about stress, it implies three ways in which stress can be coped with by the individual: avoidance, defence mechanisms and learning.

Avoidance

The framework suggests that stress is fundamentally determined by the situation rather than by the person. Although people may vary in the amount of activation they can apply before reaching the stress level, it is the events and situations that people are involved in which are the primary causes. Getting out of the situation is therefore the most obvious way of escaping stress. Inasmuch as stress is like physical pain - a functional warning signal that one is damaging oneself - then it has evolved to function through avoidance. One practical lesson therefore is that one should always heed the warnings, rather than force oneself to continue in situations which provoke anxiety. However, to people in a stressing situation, the advice to get out is much more easily given than taken. After all, if some one is frustrated in the achievement of a personally important aim, he cannot simply choose to give up; such aims are not chosen, but discovered.

In such situations, a painful process of learning which goals are realizable may be inevitable. People who are beyond freeing themselves from a stressing situation through a conscious choice will either come to such an adaptation, or find a forced avoidance in the form of a breakdown or psychosomatic illness. For those who suffer these unfortunate events, or are involved with those who do, it may be of some use and comfort to consider that even these extreme forms of stress may be functional in that they do enforce avoidance of the stressing situation, they do enforce a period of rest in which a psychological adjustment can take place and, by their nature, they stimulate a resetting of priorities and goals.

Finally, it should be noted that avoidance probably leaves the person no better or worse at coping with the offending situation, or other situations, than he was before.

Defence Mechanisms

In terms of the framework developed here, a person in a state of stress who changes to perceive less uncertainty or less importance in the outcome, or less personal influence over it, would reduce his activation level and hence avoid stress. It seems likely that such processes do operate, consciously, unconsciously or semi-consciously, to cope with stress and thus they belong to the general class of phenomena called 'defence mechanisms'. The general process of such mechanisms is to adjust the perception of reality to preserve inner balance at the expense of becoming unrealistic in relation to external realities. Four things can be said about defence mechanisms. Firstly, they operate to some degree in everybody. Secondly, if they become powerful they can result in inappropriate behaviour in situations which, in turn, exacerbate their stress-inducing features. Thirdly, their use therefore tends to leave people *less* able to cope with the situation that caused the stress. Fourthly, defence mechanisms may, however, be functional in coping with stress, since (a) the short-term respite which they buy may be necessary for survival, (b) that respite may be necessary to allow some other form of coping (avoidance or learning) to take place. It may not therefore always be constructive to confront defence mechanisms in oneself and others with reality.

Learning

The framework suggests that increasing skill decreases perceived uncertainty of the outcome of events which, in turn, reduces activation. Learning, as a process of acquiring the ability to control the outcomes in anxiety-producing situations, is therefore clearly an effective and constructive way of coping with stress that leaves the person *better* able to cope with situations that confront him. It is differences in ability and the process of learning that account for the fact that some people cope as a matter of routine with situations which reduce others to depths of anxiety, and the fact that most of us find early days in a new situation - school, job, even marriage - more stressful, in general, than later ones.

The difficulties with learning as a process of coping with stress are that it is preventative rather than remedial, it is a process which involves some uncertainties in itself, and it is a task or event which can generate anxiety and stress. Although much has been written about learning, it is not a very well understood process. However, evidence suggests that learning is most likely to occur at a level of activation which constitutes high motivation but not stress. Learning is thus a process for avoiding future stress rather than a way to cope with it in the present. For the latter, avoidance and defence mechanisms may have to function to give the person time to learn.

Another tentative conclusion about the learning process is that, in the context of acquiring abilities to cope with unfamiliar situations, it is fundamentally a process of trial and error, and of discovery. This means that the outcome is uncertain. Since it is also important and subject to influence by the individual, learning itself generates anxiety and stress.

The practical conclusion therefore is that learning is the fundamental way of overcoming stress. Avoidance and escape mechanisms may be necessary to make learning possible, and learning - for self and others - must progress naturally and at its own pace if it is not to generate anxiety in its turn.

AN ORGANIZATIONAL PERSPECTIVE

Standing back from the individual and his levels of activation, it is amusing for the outsider, and distressing for the insider, to observe simultaneous discussion of 'executive stress' and 'shopfloor tedium'. Are managers working hard, above their stress thresholds, to keep operatives and clerical workers below their motivation thresholds and in the area of boredom? Do managers programme their workers' activities in great detail to give themselves a false sense of certainty? It might be trite to answer 'Yes' to these questions too readily, but there may well be a tendency for the current industrial system to push people either into stress or tedium. If this is so, then it seems obviously sensible to try to share the activation a little more evenly in organizations so that more people can work at a level of motivation at which they perform and learn. Job enrichment at the shop floor and clerical levels tends to mean doing a lot of different tedious jobs some of the time rather than one tedious job all the time. This is not likely to lead to a significant increase in activation and motivation. The situation demands what Herzberg calls 'vertical' job enrichment rather than this more normal 'horizontal' form. The result is an involvement in the uncertainty surrounding a programmed task. How can it be improved? Is it necessary? How does it fit with other operations? How long do we need it? how do we change it?

At the other end of the spectrum, delegation is usually advocated as the means of unburdening the hard-pressed manager, and sharing his responsibility round the organization. However, where practised, delegation usually *increases* stress. The busy manager is encouraged to hand over the routine aspects of his job to assistants, and delegate the more structured of his problems to subordinates.

The time which he thus saves to think on the broader issues turns out to be time to worry about all the organization's most intractable and stress-inducing problems! The manager who delegates in this way leaves himself with a personal portfolio which has a *higher* average level of activation and stress-inducing potential. Somehow, he has got to reverse the process and delegate some of the more highly involving activities to enrich the jobs of those suffering at the other end of the activation scale.

References

1. The basic idea for this formula is derived from J F Morris' concept of 'Drama'. See J F Morris, 'Three aspects of the person in social life', in R Ruddock (ed), *Six Approaches to the Person*, Routledge and Kegan Paul, 1972.

2. A Toffler, *Future Shock*, Bodley Head, 1970.

3. R M Yerkes and J D Dodson, 'The relation of strength of stimulus to rapidity of habit-formation', *Journal of Comparative Neurology and Psychology*, Vol 18, 1908, pp 459-82.

4. J A Hammes, 'Visual discrimination learning as a function of shock, fear and task difficulty', *Journal of Comparative Neurology and Psychology*, Vol 49, 1956, pp 481-4.

5. P L Broadhurst, 'Emotionality and the Yerkes-Dodson Law', *Journal of Experimental Psychology*, Vol 54, 1957, pp 345-52.

6. J V Brady, 'Ulcers in "executive" monkeys', *Scientific American*, Vol 199, 1958, pp 95-100.

2

Stress, Success and Legitimacy

Dan Gowler and Karen Legge

It is a contemporary commonplace that social life in complex industrial societies is beset by 'stresses and strains' to an extent unknown in earlier times and simpler societies. Furthermore, and here we come to the central theme of this chapter, it is also a commonplace that managerial roles inevitably involve those concerned in situations known to induce and/or exacerbate stress.

In this chapter, we discuss the question of managerial stress from three distinct, though related, points of view. Firstly, we examine stress in relation to the *individual*. For example, we consider how stress may be generated by the way in which individuals perceive, react and adjust to their particular circumstances. Secondly, we examine stress in relation to the *managerial role*. Briefly, this view of stress is necessary since much individual behaviour in work organizations is a function of formal role playing. The point here is that this role playing, which involves the individual in a network of social relationships, often results in distressing forms of intra - and inter personal conflict. Thirdly, we discuss how stress may be generated in work organizations by the explicit and implicit use of *success criteria* - the values and frames of reference used to evaluate managerial performance. Fourthly, as suggested above, we also consider the relationships between these three perspectives (see Figure 2.1) and illustrate them through an analysis of the stressful situation which faces personnel managers attempting to establish the *legitimacy* of their activities.

Finally, we discuss how people manipulate means and ends in order to cope with their anxieties and frustrations. From this we derive a general definition of stress based on the concepts of 'mismatch' and 'coercion'.

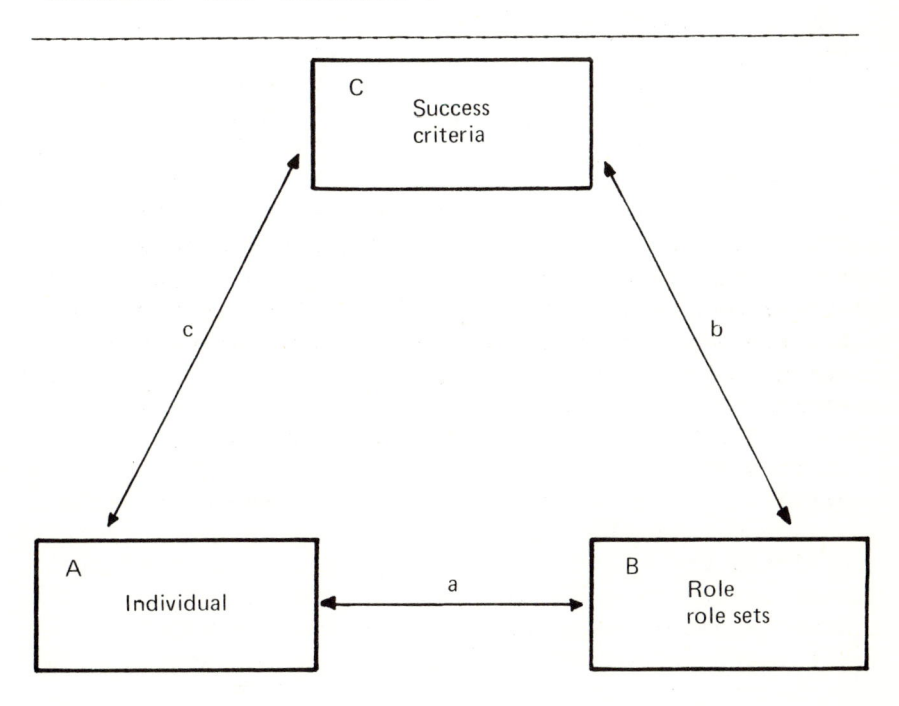

Figure 2: 1   Stress: three interrelated perspectives

THE INDIVIDUAL AND STRESS

The first element in our model is the individual or psychological aspects of stress (see box A, Figure 2.1). But this raises a fundamental problem of definition, which has to be dealt with before we can proceed with our analysis.

This problem is reflected in the difficulty of distinguishing, if there is a difference, between the terms 'anxiety' and 'stress'. It has been suggested that the problem may be resolved by treating 'stress' as an attribute of situations, whilst reserving the term 'anxiety' for the actual emotional state of the individual. Thus, on the basis of this distinction, individuals would have feelings of anxiety in stressful situations.

Unfortunately, this clear-cut distinction, though providing a satisfactory degree of terminological exactitude, conceals a number of major difficulties. First, when we say a person is anxious, we may mean that he is anxious at a given point in time and/or circumstance. On the other hand, we may mean that he is an anxious person, who shows signs of anxiety in a wide range of situations and during relatively long periods of time. In other words, anxiety might range from a temporary to a permanent condition. In the temporary state, we are likely to place emphasis on the circumstances believed to have been the cause of the transient emotional state. At the other end of the continuum - the so-called anxious person - we are likely to be more interested in characteristics of the individuals concerned, particularly those believed to make these people perceive threats and difficulties where most others do not. Our reason for making this distinction is not only to suggest that temporary states of anxiety are normal and that permanent states are not, but to raise the important question of the complex relationship between perceptions and situations. However normal or abnormal individuals might be, a situation is not stressful unless it is perceived as such.

Second, this 'perceptual' problem bedevils experimentation in this field of interest, for the subject of an experiment, say, in the arousal of anxiety may not perceive any threat or difficulty in the conditions contrived by the experimenters.(1) Furthermore, given variations in different individuals' responses to the same stimuli, it is difficult - if not impossible - to come to any firm conclusion on the matter. It is important to note that these difficulties put a question mark against such quasi-experimental situations as stress interviewing for job selection and so on, quite apart from the questionable morality of such procedures.

To summarize these points, it is difficult to isolate causality here. For example, is the anxiety felt by the manager who believes he has not the information or resources to achieve objectives, 'real' or not? Put simply, is this lack of information and resources a fact or is it that the manager's perceptions are at fault? Unfortunately, the answers to this type of question are often confused, arbitrary and founded in the prejudices of those making the judgements. This is not surprising, given the problems outlined above.

Bearing these difficulties in mind, we have to recognize that emphasis on the vexed questions of definition and causality is likely to result in little more than a dead-end debate about the priority and reality of perceptions and circumstances. However, for the purpose of dealing with such problems, we do have to make distinctions and decisions about the emotional state of individuals, eg anxiety, and about the nature of the difficulties in their situations, eg stressful circumstances, even though we are aware that such conclusions may be unreal and unfair. Moreover, practical problems make it necessary for us to develop theories about the relationship between anxiety states and stressful circumstances, even though we are aware that they may be both speculative and spurious.

There is, however, a useful approach to the understanding of the complex interrelationships between the individual's perceptions, situation and anxiety, which is through the concept of 'social role'.

ROLES, INDIVIDUALS AND STRESS

In a sense, role theory provides a conceptual* link between the concepts of stress and anxiety as discussed above.(2) First, the idea of role focuses attention on the fact that an individual's thoughts, values, feelings and behaviours are influenced by the rights and duties attached to a given social position or role (see arrow a, Figure 2.1). Second, through the concept of 'role set',+ it provides a framework with which to examine the structure of the situation in which the individual is embedded. In other words, the concepts of role and role set link the individual with social structure.

Thus, using role theory, we would expect stressful situations to occur when, for example,

1 an individual is confronted with conflicting demands from members of his *different* role sets. For example, when a manager's superordinate (a member of his occupational role set) requests his attendance at an after-hours meeting, when his wife (a member of his domestic role set) requests that he comes home early to meet visitors whom they invited for the evening.(4)

2 an individual is confronted with conflicting demands from *within* one of his role sets. For example, when a manager refuses to allow his subordinates time off to attend a union meeting, on the belief that such activities should not take

---
* We use the word 'conceptual' to emphasize that a social role is a theoretical construct, ie a representation or model of reality.
+ Defined here as 'all the role-relationships that a person has with the people in other roles with whom he interacts in the performance of his role(s)'.(3)

place 'in the firm's time'.

3 an individual is unclear about (or rejects) the expectations and behaviours appropriate to any one or more of his roles, which may also involve problems within and between his various role sets. These difficulties often occur when managers (and others) move into new roles, eg through promotion and transfer, or when they have their existing roles modified in some way, eg as a result of technological or organizational change.

These examples of the difficulties generated by various forms of role conflict and ambiguity are necessary but not sufficient causes of anxiety. For the difficulties outlined above only really become stressful when (a) an individual has to choose and act in the situation of conflict and/or ambiguity, eg when the manager, cited in case 1 above, has to enforce his decision, (b) when an individual is unclear about the sanctions, ie rewards and punishments, that are related to his decisions and acts. Of course, the situation is likely to become even more stressful when (a) and (b) are compounded, eg when managers have to make decisions and act in circumstances where the outcome of, and rewards for these behaviours are uncertain.

It is important to note here that roles and role sets are defined and evaluated by formal and informal systems of control which operate in the work situation. Through the various forms of performance appraisal, these roles and role sets are then related to organizational success criteria, eg reduced unit costs, increased profits, higher productivity and output, improved standards of quality, better industrial relations and so on. These evaluations of managerial role playing are then related to rewards, eg to salaries, fringe benefits, status symbols and promotion.

These relationships between individuals, roles and success criteria (see arrows a,b and c, Figure 2.1) jointly contribute to the stressses in the manager's environment. Thus, in the light of these comments, we believe it necessary to discuss in more detail the relationship between stress and success criteria, particularly as it pertains to managerial role playing.

SUCCESS CRITERIA AND STRESS

In our view, organizational success criteria induce anxiety by two processes, which are represented by arrows b and c in Figure 2.1. Most organizations either implicitly or explicitly enshrine their success criteria in their goals and objectives. In other words, these goals and objectives involve certain indicators of organizational success, such as rate of growth, market share, return on capital, the quality of goods and services provided for customers and clients, or the firm's industrial relations record, which, through the network of controls and roles, are transformed into both the reasons for and the measures of managerial action. Of course, this is a rather simple-minded view of the way in which organizations function, and much recent research has given us a much more complex view of these processes. (5) However, despite this caveat, action plans generally contain an indication of what the managers concerned are supposed to achieve, whether it is expressed in terms of sales, budgets, or less tangible objectives, as 'to design an effective development programme for a specific group of managers',

As suggested above, these objectives also become the criteria for evaluating a manager's performance and, thereby, organizational success criteria are transformed into managerial success criteria. An example of an explicit formalization of this transformation is what is sometimes termed 'Management by Objectives' (MBO).(6) But MBO also represents the way in which organizational success criteria may redefine managerial roles (see arrow b, Figure 2.1), as formal role requirements may be rewritten in terms of what is considered either desirable or feasible in the light of new formulations of the success criteria. Even without the formalization of MBO schemes, changing ideas about organizational success criteria - either in their form or the manner by which they are to be achieved - influence both the design and evaluation of jobs. But where does stress come in all this?

As commented above, work organizations do not operate in the mechanistic manner suggested by the smooth transformation of organizational objectives into managerial action. In practice, this transformation is influenced by a number of factors including, for example, the organizational politics engaged in by changing coalitions of managers,(7) who often operate with different and conflicting ideas about organizational ends and means. Consequently, many managers find themselves in the stressful situation where both short - and long-term objectives are subject to constant revision, and the means adopted to achieve them are constantly modified, or abandoned altogether.

These comments raise the question, why is it that such circumstances create managerial anxiety? For a rational response to such situations might be to adopt a fatalistic or unconcerned attitude to these difficulties. The answer to this question introduces the second of the two processes mentioned above - that involving the relationship between the individual and organizational success criteria (see arrow c, Figure 2.1). Ultimately, it would appear that a situation becomes stressful *when an individual feels unable to deal with the demands it makes upon him, while at the same time he also feels that he must.* In other words, an individual is likely to be made anxious by his *inability to achieve,* whether it be in terms of his own or others' definition of achievement. This view is supported by the studies of managerial stress that have indicated that either 'too many' or 'too few' demands may create feelings of frustration, resentment and anxiety.(8)

It must be emphasized here that the anxiety created by perceived under-achievement is not only a question of *external* rewards and punishments, such as job tenure, salaries and promotion, but also a matter of *internal* needs to achieve. In other words, individuals do not wish to achieve solely to be rewarded by promotion and salary but have to satisfy the demands of self-image and self-esteem. Furthermore, such evidence as we have suggests that workloads, levels of self-esteem and feelings of guilt and anxiety are in fact closely related. For example, one study reports that

> Managers and workers who were high on perceptions of job pressure reported feeling nervous and anxious in the presence of superiors, being submissive and apologetic when they had done something wrong, and often thinking that they were not as good as other people. They reported often asking themselves whether or not they had 'done right', being depressed by their own feelings of unworthiness, and feeling that people disapproved of them...(9)

Further,

> Managers who were high on job pressure reported worrying a lot about their ability to succeed and that they recalled for a long time with distress those occasions in which they had made a poor showing.(10)

To summarize: managers (and others) are likely to feel anxious when they experience a mismatch between their need for and ability to achieve. This mismatch is a function of situational factors, eg organizational success criteria and the demands they make upon those concerned, plus the nature of external motivators, such as salaries and promotions, and internal personality traits, eg levels of competativeness, perseverance and self-esteem. Finally, it is important to note that all the considerations outlined in this summary are permeated by our culture's emphasis on the value of high levels of individual and collective effort.(11)

STRESS AND THE SPECIALIST

Up to this point, we have emphasized the anxiety aroused by the *individual's* inability to achieve in terms of the success criteria that define and evaluate his performance in the managerial role. Before we return to this issue, we shall consider the situation where the *role itself* has difficulties in relation to the organizational success criteria (see arrow b, Figure 2.1). For there are roles which may appear to the individual concerned as particularly loaded against even the smallest measure of success.

One example of such a circumstance has been defined by Kahn *et al* as a situation of *role ambiguity*, where there is a 'discrepancy between the information available to the person and that which is required for adequate performance of his role'.(12) This is a well-known source of managerial anxiety and we do not pursue this issue any further here. But what of situations where ambiguity exists about the very success criteria, which are supposed to provide the point of reference for both the definition and evaluation of role performance? We suggest that when this form of ambiguity pertains, the roles - and, by association, their incumbents - are seen to lack *legitimacy*. Put simply, such roles would lack *authority*, since the powers (rights and duties) attached to them are likely to be unclear and, as such, unacceptable.*

Such stressful circumstances may be illustrated by reference to the difficulties of certain specialists who have now become textbook examples of these stressful 'illegitimate' roles. With this in mind, we shall examine in some detail the almost classic case of the *personnel specialist*. To begin, we refer to a recent study.
_____
* Thus sociologists often define 'authority' as 'legitimate power'.(13)

which

> ...found that the role of the personnel department was not clearly defined. There was a lack of clear definition in management's expectation of the personnel function, and a corresponding reticence among personnel managers to indicate what they felt this role should be. The authors of the report felt that the unclear definition of personnel responsibilities was the root of many of the problems found in the personnel department. This lack of definition applied to the purpose of the personnel function, the relationship of the personnel function to line management and the relationship to other departments on personnel matters.(14)

Put bluntly, these observations indicate how difficult it is to relate the personnel function (and roles) to organizational success criteria, since there is a real problem in determining how 'personnel' does, or should, contribute to ultimate aims and objectives. For example, it is not easy to see the *direct* relationship, say, between the successful implementation of a new job evaluation scheme and profits, growth, market share and so on.

In more general terms, the personnel specialist is more likely to be concerned with *means*, eg the recruitment and training of staff, than with *ends*,* eg corporate strategy, in situations where there is difficulty in determining the relationship between the means and ends. It does not take too much imagination to see what stresses this situation generates for the personnel manager. Moreover, in the light of these comments, it is easy to see how difficult it is for personnel specialists to establish acceptable (legitimate) roles in many work

---

*This fact is often reflected in the view that personnel managers 'should only provide a service' and that such specialists should be 'on tap not on top'.

organizations.

In contrast, many other managerial functions engage in activities that have tangible and measurable outcomes, and are therefore more 'legitimate' in the sense that they are both *believed and seen to be necessary* for organizational growth and survival. For example, the activities of a production manager can be evaluated in terms of the quantity and quality of output. Another example of such legitimate activities is the marketing manager, who may be evaluated in terms of volume of sales, market share and so on. Of course, the most legitimate roles, at least in terms of the clarity of organizational ends and means, are those of the financial specialists. For they have the privileged, some might say 'priestly' role of being the arbiter of the means - ends relationship, ie they are called upon to evaluate in financial terms the appropriateness of ends, means, and the relationship between them.

We do appreciate, however, that anxiety may be generated by certainty as well as uncertainty. Thus, production, marketing and financial specialists might argue that, given relatively unequivocal standards of evaluation, they are unlikely to avoid criticism and retribution if they do not measure up to expectations. They might also argue that the personnel specialists, who cannot so easily be brought to account, may use the ambiguity of the relationship between their activities and organizational aims and objectives to escape or avoid evaluation and accountability.

These observations apart, the personnel specialist suffers from another 'structural' factor, that is that the personnel *function* is ommipresent and, as such, involved in every other function, whether it be production, marketing, finance and so on. This is because the people involved in these various activities have to be recruited, trained, motivated and rewarded, all of which involve the personnel function, if not the personnel specialist and his department. Yet, paradoxically, it is this study ommipresent nature of the personnel function which makes it difficult for those in specialist personnel roles to lay exclusive claims to success (or failure) in those 'personnel' activities that might be regarded as tangible and measurable. Thus, fewer strikes and stoppages, low absenteeism and labour turnover, which can all be measured and might also be accepted as success criteria for personnel managers, are not necessarily considered as such. For example, line managers frequently claim credit for, say, reduced absenteeism and labour turnover, and it cannot be denied that such claims are often well founded. Consequently, this diffusion of the personnel function into line management and other managerial roles may result, if taken to its extreme, in the suggestion that the personnel function does not require a departmental presence.

Again to summarize: we have discussed the idea that difficulty in establishing unambiguous and acceptable success criteria for the performance of personnel roles has important implications for those concerned. These ideas relate to our earlier assertions that an individual is likely to feel anxious when he cannot achieve, either in terms of his own success criteria (see arrow c, Figure 2.1) or those attached to his occupational role (arrow b).

MEANS, ENDS AND COPING BEHAVIOURS

We now develop the ideas discussed in the previous section and consider some further aspects of the inability to develop 'unambiguous and acceptable success criteria' for certain specialist roles, particularly that of the personnel specialist. Furthermore, we shall discuss how individuals cope with the stresses and strains found in such circumstances.

First, as already suggested, the problem of success criteria makes it difficult, if not impossible, for personnel specialists to establish legitimate roles

in their organizations. This is not, however, the
only source of anxiety, for these roles are also
likely to be seen as unimportant and therefore of
relatively low status. This low status is likely to
be reflected in salary and promotion prospects, which
not only reinforce the poor image of the roles concerned but create other sources of anxiety. Moreover,
given this low status, individuals transferred to,
say, the personnel department may perceive the move
as a penalty for poor performance, which again
reinforces the 'image' problems of the department.

How individuals in personnel and other specialist
roles deal with these problems reveals what are
termed *coping* behaviours, which themselves throw
light on the nature of anxiety. These behaviours
also help to resolve some of the definitional
problems discussed at the beginning of this chapter.

There is, first, the coping behaviour that we term
routinization, by which the manager concerned
transforms means into ends, thus resolving any
ambiguity in the relationship between means and ends.
Why do we call this routinization? Briefly, we have
observed that the transformation of means into ends
is achieved by the manager concentrating his time
and energy on those routine, everyday activities
which are, in effect, ends in themselves in that they
would have to be undertaken, whatever the organization
and whatever its ends. An example of routinization
is provided by the personnel manager who allocates
most of his time to routine service activities, eg
canteens, health, welfare work and wage and salary
administration.

Another form of coping behaviour is that we term
'innovation', in which the stresses and strains in
the situation result in the introduction of new
activities. One such type of behaviour is that we
term *'conformist innovation'*, the individuals
concerned behaving in an entrepreneurial fashion and,
in this case, attempting to change means in order to
match them against accepted ends. Hence the use of

the adjective 'conformist'. To take yet another example from the personnel department, conformist innovation occurs when personnel specialists introduce techniques such as cost benefit analysis and human resource accounting, which are attempts to bring certain of their activities in line with unambiguous and acceptable success criteria, in this case the financial criteria.

Innovation also includes what we term *'deviant innovation'*, in which the stresses and strains of the situation encourage those concerned to change *both* means and ends. The American sociologist Robert Merton describes the rejection of both prescribed means and success goals or ends as either *retreatism* or *rebellion*.(15) Retreatism is the type of adaption to social life characterized by the activities of, for example, tramps and drug adicts. Rebellion, which appears to be similar to retreatism, is in effect quite different since it involves the idea of *purposeful change*, while retreatism does not entail innovation. However, our notion of deviant innovation - which is similar to Merton's idea of rebellion - is exemplified by attempts to establish personnel management as a profession. The point we are making here is that the professional does claim, among other things, the privilege to operate with means and ends that are not necessarily the same as those prescribed by the organization that employs him. This independent status is reflected in the hospital doctor's claim to 'clinical freedom' and the university professor's claim to 'academic freedom'.

Thus, if the personnel manager can establish himself as a professional in the organization that employs him, he will be able to introduce a new means - ends relationship free from the ambiguities and low status described above. It must be noted, however, that the professional does have problems with this 'independent status', which are often represented in the literature as a classic example of role conflict. For he often finds himself 'torn' between his obligations to his employers and those owed to his profession.

The last point, with its emphasis on dissonance and conflict, returns us to the question of stress and anxiety. For the common denominator of coping behaviours is the attempt to resolve *a perceived mismatch** in the situation concerned, eg between ends and means. As commented above, this throws some light on the vexed question, 'what is stress?' Our analysis suggests that stress is present when the individual perceives a mismatch in his circumstances, eg between prescribed role behaviours (means) and organizational success criteria (ends), and where there is also present a coercive factor, eg the 'need to achieve', which compels him to resolve the mismatch concerned.

In conclusion, in terms of this 'mismatch theory', the 'anxiety-prone' individual is likely to be one who perceives more mismatches in his environments than others and/or experiences more compulsion to resolve them than others. Finally, it seems to us that these ideas warrant further discussion and research.(16)

References

1 See, for example, E E Levitt, *The Psychology of Anxiety*, Paladin, 1971, pp 104-116. (First published by Bobbs-Merrill, New York, 1967.)

2 R L Kahn, D M Wolfe, R P Quinn, J D Snoek and R A Rosenthal, *Organizational Stress: Studies in Role Conflict and Ambiguity*, Wiley, New York, 1964; S F Nadel, *The Theory of Social Structure*, Cohen and West, 1957.

3 For a fuller discussion of this concept, see, R K Merton, 'The role-set: problems in sociological theory', *British Journal of Sociology*, Vol 8, No 2, June 1957, pp 106-20.

---

*We are indebted to Professor John Morris for this useful insight.

4   See Chapter 4 in which the question of stress and marital relationships is developed.

5   See, for example, R M Cyert and J G March, *A Behavioral Theory of The Firm*, Prentice-Hall, Englewood Cliffs, N J, 1963.

6   See, for example, J W Humble, *Improving Management Performance*, Management Publications, BIM, 1960; also P F Drucker, *The Practice of Management*, Mercury Books, 1961, (First published by Heinemann, 1955.)

7   See, R M Cyert and J G March, op cit; also A Pettigrew, *The Politics of Organizational Decision-Making*, Tavistock, 1973; J Boissevain, *Friends of Friends-Networks, Manipulators and Coalitions*, Basil Blackwell, 1974.

8   E Jaques, *Equitable Payment*, Heinemann Educational Books, 1961.

9   V E Buck, *Working Under Pressure*, Staples Press, 1972, p 98.

10 ibid, p 98.

11 D C McClelland, *The Acheiving Society*, Van Nostrand, Princeton, N J, 1961.

12 R L Kahn et al, op cit, p 73.

13 M Weber, *The Theory of Social and Economic Organization*, Free Press of Glencoe, New York, 1964, pp 324-33. (Translated by A M Henderson and T Parsons, Oxford University Press, New York, 1947.)

14 G Ritzer and H M Trice, *An Occupation in Conflict - A Study of the Personnel Manager*, Cornell University Press, Ithaca, NY, 1969, p 65.

15 R K Merton, *Social Theory and Social Structure*, Free Press of Glencoe, New York, 1949, p 133.

16 A form of 'mismatch' theory has already been presented in the concept of 'cognitive dissonance'. See L Festinger, *A Theory of Cognitive Dissonance*, Row, Peterson, New York, 1957; also D Gowler and K Legge, 'Occupational role development - Parts 1 and 2', *Personnel Review*, Vol 1, Nos 2 and 3, Spring and Summer 1972, pp 12-27, pp 58-73.

3

Managerial Stress and the 'Cross of Relationships'

John Morris

'Managerial stress' readily evokes a flow of images, many of them cliches. Managers in smoke-filled rooms, wheeling and dealing, the ulcers quietly forming in churning stomachs. Managers flying urgently over time-zones, disrupting the delicate balance of sleeping and waking, building up irritability and depression that lasts for days of vital meetings which they dare not defer. Managers held accountable by powerful people that they hardly know for results that they could do little or nothing to influence. Managers displaced from their jobs by boardroom politics, with no management trade unions to appeal to. Managers being ruthlessly grilled in the hot seats of television studios, watched by critical millions, including their own colleagues and subordinates.

'Stress' in all these contexts means much more than

a heavy workload,(1) though 'overwork' is still a
favourite common-sense explanation of stress reactions
running from ulcers to depression and even suicide.
It means a combination of uncertainty, an important
issue, and a sense of being held accountable for
whatever happens. This combination can best be
summarized as a concern about personal failure, a
breakdown in one's sense of control over events.
This concern can lead to many reactions, most of them
intensely disagreeable for those experiencing them.
This is why stress has such an ugly ring, especially
when we connect it with managers, who are powerful
enough to spread some of their concern over failure
to their associates.(2) The possibilities have an
all-too-familiar sound: anxiety, tension,
irritability, rage, despair, apathy.

These responses to stress are part of the infinite
variety of the human condition. Some far-sighted
observers would say that managerial stress is only a
tiny part of the great mountain of human suffering.
They might add that managers are more fortunate than
most men, because they have skilled support for their
stress. The stress of the poor and powerless is dumb:
the manager has the mastery of language. All this is
true, but managers are here to stay, and anything
that enables them to keep their abilities, their
energies and their goodwill clear and bright seems
worth while to examine. These notes suggest that
managerial stress can be illuminated and to some
extent relieved by considering the implications of
some simple models of managerial relationships and
managerial tasks.

SIMPLIFYING THE MANAGERIAL SITUATION

Let us make a start with some brisk managerial
assertions that seem to be common-sense models of
simplicity. 'Always let your boss know what you're
planning to do.' 'Never take your worries home.'
'Remember that today's halo will be tomorrow's
millstone.' 'Let the other man do the worrying'.

These are some of the ways in which managers identify sources of stress, propose rules for coping, and philosophize about life - all in a few homely phrases. They are managerial in the sense that they do not take much time out from action, and point back to action pretty quickly.

Taking the cue from such phrases, it seems useful to look for those influences that the manager has to deal with throughout the course of his working life. These flood in from four directions; from his seniors, and particularly his immediate boss, from his immediate juniors, from his working colleagues and from a variety of people outside the organization. These are not the only directions of information and influence, but they are most important. I shall dramatize the situation by leaving out everyone and everything in the organization apart from the manager and these four lines of relationship. We can call this *'the cross of relationships'* (3) and, with one other model, the *'four-task model'*, it will play a leading part in these notes.

Figure 3: 1   The cross of relationships

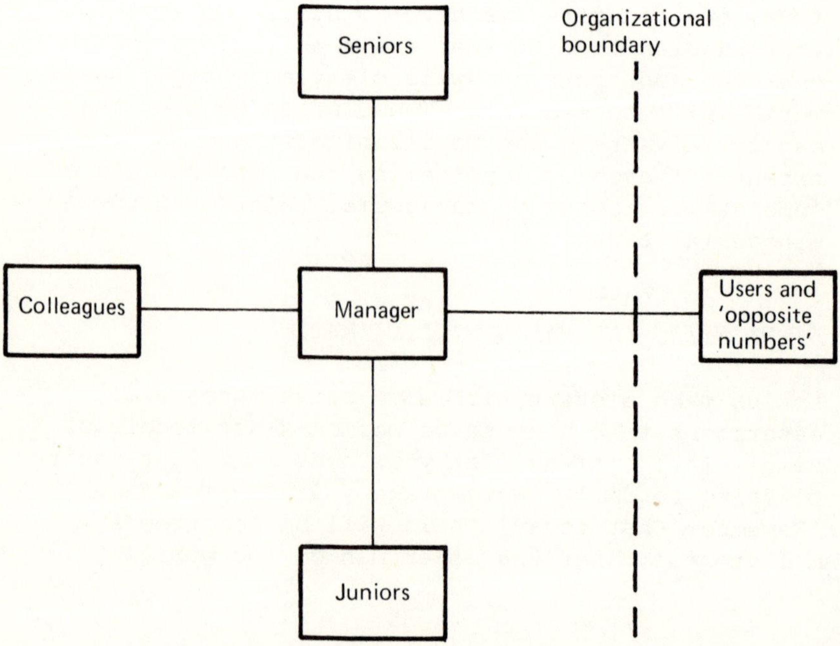

The cross (Figure 3.1) looks very different from the usual organization chart, which shows a pyramid of management and operative positions, divided by horizontal lines into status levels and by vertical lines into reporting relationships. In the cross of relationships, it is possible to look at a single management position and to remind ourselves that every manager, from the most junior to the most senior, sees himself as being at the centre of such a cross. (Those in junior management in large organizations might be forgiven for assuming that the chief executive, many levels above them, has no upwards reporting line, except perhaps to the Almighty. The executive knows different, and often feels greatly oppressed by his masters, whether government, shareholders, or even bigger organizations.)

The cross is a powerful simplifying device, admittedly simpler than reality can afford to be. But it serves as a useful way of helping the manager, who places himself at its centre, to think of what is being done to him by the flood of activities and expectations reaching him along the four arms. He can also, we hope, reflect on what he is doing to others by his own activities and expectations. Unexamined stress can make us do very unreasonable things.

Each of the four arms of the cross is subject to trends in the pattern of relationships: authority and influence are increasingly being attacked, examined and freshly evaluated. Some of these trends seem to go in contradictory directions: for example, demands from junior managers for clear guidelines are linked with equally strong demands for independence. We shall briefly examine some of the leading trends in each arm, and then summarize some of the issues that seem to emerge from the cross as a whole. We shall hope to find sufficient coherence to encourage the manager who believes that reflection on his predicament can lead to some powerful simplifications.

Trends in Relations with Seniors

The word 'senior' itself is expressive of a trend. Managers seem increasingly uncertain about how to treat the people above them in the organizational hierarchy. 'Boss' is informally used, but in a sense that suggests that the boss has no right to be bossy. Textbooks in organization still talk creakingly of 'superiors' and 'subordinates', but such terms seem far distant from day-to-day working relationships.

It seems clear that seniors are often not sufficiently in command of their own situation to issue clear and durable guidelines to their juniors.(4) They can indicate particular activities to do, monitor performance, switch other people's activities in an emergency, but they find it difficult to work successfully to long-term plans, though many of them are convinced that this would be desirable, if only *their* seniors would commit themselves to the long term!

Relations with seniors become increasingly complicated in large organizations with the rapid growth of specialist functions, each of which takes a sophisticated slice of organizational activities and promises to improve overall effectiveness by dealing with this slice with its specialist skills. Each of these slices - personnel, finance, accounting, various kinds of technical functions, computers and so on - has to achieve its effectiveness through those who are handling the main flow of work through the organization. Much of this influence is exerted in relation to colleagues. But the decision to use specialist services and, particularly, the decision to add a new specialism, is usually made by top management, and then becomes a powerful constraint flowing through the top arm of the cross.

A related trend, but in a contrary direction, is towards seniors trying to integrate their diverse activities, so that their own uncertainties and fears of failure are kept in bounds. This often takes the form of constant reorganizations, each aspiring after

the right blend of sufficient complexity to be
realistic and enough simplicity to be comprehensible.
Management by Objectives, Profit Centre Management,
Management by Exception and many other programmed
systems of management (sometimes degenerating into
'packages') have all played their part in helping
top managers feel that they are in control. More
influentially and all-pervasively, financial control
systems come to the forefront and provide powerful
methods for converting the manifold activities of
organizational life into a limited number of ratios.
This soon leads to confrontations with another all-
pervasive system in the organization, the 'culture'
as a set of assumptions, customs, habits and
expectations that provides a basis for all the other
management systems. Such confrontations occur in the
cross of relationships, particularly with juniors.(5)

Trends in Relations with Juniors

If we think of the manager at the centre of the cross
as a middle-aged middle manager in a large organization,
the trends that he is likely to experience on the arm
pointing down to juniors are of intense, volatile and
to some extent contradictory expectations. The young
men, the under-thirties, expect more independence,
but often want firm guidelines within which to
practise it. They see themselves as professional
managers, with a licence to drive over organizational
boundaries if their career points that way. Yet many
of the more ambitious among them hope to rise above
their professional specialisms, as computer managers,
research managers, personnel managers, even economists
and accountants, and establish themselves as general
managers. And the professional generalist is still
a difficult kind of manager to define, or even to
recognize clearly. At one extreme, he can be a hard-
headed integrator (6) around a single impersonal
value, such as growth through acquisition, or earnings
per share. At the other, he may pursue a vision of
the organization as an agent of fundamental human
values, a peaceful community growing into a common-
wealth.

Juniors with expectations of this diversity can be rich sources of stress. How can their managers succeed in managing them? One apparently attractive prospect is to move from being a manager to being a colleague, a rather senior kind of colleague admittedly, but an elder brother rather than an organizational parent. But what will the older managers higher up the organization think about this? The interrelation between the upper and lower arms of the cross, both nominally focusing on the management of authority, can become difficult to balance, and it is no wonder that experienced managers are fascinated and puzzled by problems of 'delegation', 'devolution' and 'participation'. Some of them wonder whether these are the agreeable disguises under which lurk abdication, humiliation and fragmentation.

Trends in Relations with Colleagues

Colleagues come in all shapes and sizes: some are line managers, seeing themselves as practical people with a job to be done and with far too little time, money and other resources to accomplish it. Others are members of the growing band of specialists already mentioned, with professional careers to pursue. (7) In many ways, the manager's relations with his colleagues are the most relaxed yet constructive activities of the whole cross of relationships. Yet, here too, the trends are complex. The growing emphasis on performance and 'results' may lead to colleagues being set against one another as rivals (a common tendency in the sales function). Some organizations recruit more young managers than they believe they will have room for, and leave them to pit themselves against one another. And specialist barriers of skill and language may lead to failures of understanding between managers on the same status level. They will be colleagues in name only.

Yet when all the inhibiting factors have been mentioned, working groups of colleagues seem to be very effective in coming up with new ideas and progressing them to the pilot stage. **'Project management'** has become a distinctive style of management, usually with open lines of communication and easily crossed boundaries.(8) Not only do these project groups rate highly on the professional standards of competence and integrity, they are havens of warmth in the dispersed large organization. (Some would argue that one of the few merits of large-scale organization, from the human point of view, is its ability to sustain project groups as a regular way of working for part of the organization.)

Trends in Relations with Users and 'Opposite Numbers

As large-scale organization has grown, more attention has been given to maintaining the internal environment. This can sometimes give rise to nightmarish visions of sprawling bureaucratic monsters, preoccupied with their stability, and insensitive to the needs of those who provide the flows of funds that keep them alive. But the same trends that produce internal diversity also produce a welter of external links. The homely contacts with users that are characteristic of small-scale organizations are replaced by marketing, merchandizing, distribution channels, as well as a variety of specialist lines of selling.

Some of these external links are slow-moving and inclined to regard themselves as one-way channels, from the productive services to the user. As the costs of sophisticated services have mounted, many users are attracted by innovations that seem to go back to an earlier era, when the user and provider belonged to the same community, and the user was able to provide for many of his own needs. 'Do it yourself' home improvement activities and materials, discount warehouses, car-assembly kits, self-service petrol stations, mail-order agencies all involve, along with many other developments, the user as a provider, at a reduced cost.

Yet the big organizations have been sensitive to this trend, and often mobilize their vast resources with great agility to enter these new markets. Users who are their own providers become more like miniature organizations than like individual users, and in this respect overlap with the growing number of 'opposite numbers' - the people in other organizations who work as external linkages, in union negotiations, trade associations, government agencies and consultancies. If we insist that every exchange can be fitted into the 'provider-user' framework, then these are intermediate users, part of the extended chain of procurement and provision that is the hallmark of the modern interactive economy.

An important aspect of these working relationships, however, is that they provide managers who are transacting over the boundaries of their organizations with concrete, tangible experience of how life is lived outside one's home territory. Some of the opposite numbers will be 'big league', other many be minor league, yet making proportionally larger profits and treating their managers more idiosyncratically and more generously.

A manager can use these relationships as contacts for progressing his own movements around the managerial career system, which is rapidly growing as an international network, fostered by multinational organizations which need cosmopolitans, (9) by professional institutions which have aspirations to international status, and by supporting institutions such as placement agencies (private and public) and specialized education and training establishments.

It is conventional to regard a proliferation of external links as stressful. After all, boundaries provide security; they are defences against the anxiety that is another name for fear of failure. External links can flood a person with diverse and contradictory standards, sources of information, hopes and fears. Maybe this is so. External relationships are often more guarded than those on the three internal arms of the cross. But the stark simplicity

of the cross must not be allowed to deny that this
rich complexity of the external arm can easily include
friendships and professional contacts that are the
most meaningful aspects of a manager's life.
Competition and negotiation are the commonplace of
commercial relationships. But even these can, and do,
have room for conviviality, an establishment of a
basis of mutual trust without which competition and
negotiation turn ugly, and swiftly get out of hand.

Bringing the Four Arms into Balance

If the manager at the centre of his cross is to
succeed in managing the stress that four complex and
changing sets of relationships bring him day by day,
he must find ways of balancing their respective
claims. This must clearly be a dynamic balance. At
more than one point in the foregoing discussion of
trends, comment has been made on contrasting or
contradictory tendencies. But are there some common
patterns that can serve as a basis for achieving a
balance? I believe that there are at least four.

> The rejection of arbitrary power, whether it takes
> the form of the dead hand of bureaucracy or the
> more frightening form of a tyrant.
> The related move to professionalism as a self-
> respecting but unpretentious way of getting
> socially valuable work done competently and with
> integrity.
> The desire to bring specialized competence into
> meaningful relation to fundamental values, such
> as peace, commonwealth and community.
> A desire for a personally satisfying and productive
> career, that may well cross organizational and
> specialist boundaries.

These four themes are perhaps most clearly seen among
young managers working in the development functions
of large, sophisticated organizations. In order to
survive and grow purposefully, such organizations
have elaborated a system of conscious adaption to the
ever-changing environment. Because they are able to

61

influence resource markets and product markets, they have to plan their acquisition and use of resources intelligently. Over the years, an overlapping set of professional specialisms have emerged, most of them growing out of the mainstream operating functions. Thus, oversimplifying somewhat to get a clearer focus, we can see the research scientist growing out of attempts to develop new processes and products, overlapping with the marketing specialist who looks ahead to future sales opportunities. The personnel function, traditionally concerned with keeping a stable balance in the human aspects of organization, starts to recognize the needs for organizational development, with associated changes in management style and job design. New forms of financial management emerge, ranging from management accounting to new institutions for funding expansion. Operational research applies systematic quantitative techniques to large-scale problems of production and distribution control, and then begins to see the implications of the cybernetic approach to organization, with its awareness of the all-pervasiveness of systems, whose viability must never be taken for granted.

The cross of relationships is a useful device for examining the four directions of activity and expectation, flowing to and from a single manager, viewed as an individual subsystem, constantly exposed to stress whenever the flows exceed his capacity for effective response. Now that we have made the distinction between development activities and maintenance activities, it is possible to elaborate the cross of relationships slightly to suggest that every system has four overlapping tasks:

To keep things going along established lines, using its resources effectively to meet internal and external requirements.
To do new things, partly to survive in a changing environment and partly to satisfy the system's interests in developing.
To cope with failures arising from a mismatch between the system's capacity and the demands

placed on it.
To bring these three tasks into an effective balance.

Grouping the activities of a system in this way, and switching back from this rather bloodless language to talking about managerial stress, we can see that the manager is constantly trying to balance the development and maintenance tasks,(10) without losing balance and being pushed into breakdown.

An important implication of the two models we have used is that the manager must balance a set of diverse activities if he is to manage stress. In the cross of relationships, he must balance the claims of his seniors, his juniors, his colleagues and external contacts. Within these, he must find an acceptable balance between development, maintenance and coping with failure. To some extent, he will be helped in defining the boundaries of his work by the existing shape of the organization. But the most serious weakness of organizations in their present form seems to be their relative insensitivity to individual needs for integration and balance.

Why is this? One important reason seems to be that organizations have gone through a phase of rapid growth that has exposed them to intense stress. Vast numbers of organizations have broken down totally, and their fragments have been incorporated in other organizations. Trouble-shooting has been a continuing task of managers at all levels, not least the top level which, in the organizational textbooks, is supposed to be calmly planning the next ten or twenty years. The struggle to survive has led many organizations to focus on economic or technical measures of performance, and these in turn have made it difficult to see that an organization is a social invention for the satisfaction of user and provider needs. The pursuit of economic and technical 'economies of scale' has inflated the total size of organizations enormously, and produced the current sharp reaction against the two traditional methods of handling big systems: autocracy and bureaucracy.

We seem to be groping now with two related conceptions: first, the manager as moving from specialized professional competence to becoming a professional generalist; second, the organization as a set of human beings who are searching for a new form of community, of which the organization would be a meaningful part.

As we reflect on these, it quickly becomes apparent that the new community will have a warm feeling for development rather than uncontrolled growth, and a recognition that continuity is not only one important property of intelligence but also of love, and skill. Above all, there is a recognition of the need for wholeness, not as finality or completeness, but as interconnection and identity.

In a sentence, then, we become more able to manage stress by increasing the part played by love, intelligence and skill in organizational life and by decreasing the part played by manipulation and unilateral control. The rest of this chapter expands the sentence under the heading: Learning to manage stress.

LEARNING TO MANAGE STRESS

The starting point in learning to manage stress is the recognition of the need to do something about it, usually in one's self, and the belief that something can be done. Then the trick is to *make the situation visible*. This is always done by representing it. My own preference, which seems to be fairly common, is to do this spatially, as a design or 'model'.

The two models offered and discussed in this chapter show one way of looking at the sources of managerial stress. They enable the individual manager to see how his personal predicament is part of a general situation, and this provides some measure of comfort. As the saying goes: 'A trouble shared is a trouble halved.' But the clarity of the models also allows some useful questions to be asked. Are the models picking up the most important aspects of the situation that one is confronting? Can they be improved? After all, we have made no claims for the models as *desirable*, as prescriptions of how things ought to be. All that we have claimed is they represent, in a simplified form, some leading aspects of the way in which organizations are actually set up and managed. Our study of trends is not suggesting that they ought to be happening, only that they are, and have to be reckoned with. But let me play fair. As I move towards these final recommendations, the note of value judgement will be increasingly heard.

An important element that is missing from many managers' views of life is the tendency of people to elaborate their working lives into a satisfying community with a recognizable and valued culture. People in many formal models of organization are disembodied into 'users' and 'providers', or made even more impersonal by being called 'markets' and 'personnel' - even 'manpower'. Our models have focused attention on the organization as a network of human relationships, within which people not only have information to pass, and skill to use, but *values and interests to express.*

Now comes the vital point in the sequence from the point of view of managerial effectiveness - the manager must use his analysis of the situation to move into action. What, he can ask himself, would be an improvement on what I am doing now? What would give greater control, and less fear of failure? One possibility is to move to a region of activity in which he has greater skill, since skill is a personal-control factor. Another, less direct, is to move to regions of activity in which he has greater interest, that is, greater liking, since liking is a powerful solvent of fear. Since skill and liking are often linked together, however loosely, it is wise for him to look for a change - an improvement - that would give him the opportunity of using more skill and enjoying more interest.

All very obvious, no doubt, but the trick is to turn this obviousness into particular activities, which can themselves be related to the models and used as a basis for further improvement. Step-by-step improvement, however small the steps appear to be, is a powerful enemy of stress. The curse of stress is that it induces either paralysis or oscillation, both of which are incompatible with sustained improvement. The African proverb puts it neatly: 'If you would eat the elephant in your path, cut him up into little pieces.'

But, says the anxious or angry voice of Stress, can you persuade other people to accept this piecemeal approach, with frequent stops for self-analysis and fresh programming? You yourself have shown that the heart of management is other people, and Sartre reminds us that hell is other people. How can you deal with *their* expectations? The answer to this is surely: by finding out sympathetically but accurately what they are, and comparing them with what you would like them to be. The anxiety and fear of stress notoriously magnifies expectations, or sometimes disastrously tries to deal with them by putting one's own inflated commitments in their place, and thus making rods for one's own back. The goal of steady incremental improvement, based on recognizing the directions of other people's expectations and doing something to satisfy them, requires a manageable programme that does not destroy one as a manager or (more important) as a person. *The thing is to make proposals that one feels confident of meeting, with existing resources and based solidly on past performance, and to get these proposals firmly established as the expectations of others.* This sounds extraordinarily simple, and once it is established it becomes simple. It is the business of first recognizing that the people included in one's cross of relationships are themselves at the centre of a cross. One's senior has a senior, and one's opposite numbers have opposite numbers (who include us, seen from a different perspective to that which seems familiar and natural).

To conclude, here are some aphorisms which emerged from a series of discussions on the management of stress by experienced managers at the Manchester Business School. Some of them are limited to observations on managerial situations, other are recommendations for action. I hope that they may both summarize some of the foregoing points and suggest practical ways of dealing with intractable situations.

SOME APHORISMS ON MANAGING STRESS

1 Don't be deceived by people's facades: especially your own.
2 Being open-minded isn't the same as being empty-headed.
3 Always promise a bit less than you believe you can achieve.
4 Keep things as simple as you dare, as complex as you must.
5 Put in plenty of informal progress-pegs.
6 The man who likes everyone may not be anyone. But it's good to be liked.
7 Be kind to your job, but don't let it master you.
8 Make yourself visible but not obtrusive.
9 Never forget that your boss has a boss. So does he.
10 Someone must lead, why not you? If you pause before answering, the answer is 'No'.
11 When you are doing something new, you will be back to 'square one' more than once.
12 Never get trapped in a **corner**; if necessary, make your own doors.
13 Remember that everyone loves a good-humoured victim.
14 Displaying a little intelligence takes you a long way; a lot becomes oppressive.

15 Always be as honest as people can stand.
16 When people are angry, they forget who you are. Remind them it's you.
17 Proposals put forward airily can be deflated without embarrassment.
18 People are more complex than things, so why spend so much time on things?
19 If you don't do it now, when will you?
20 Procedures start as elastic bands, and end up as barbed-wire fences.
21 Only cattle are restrained indefinitely by barbed wire.

References

1 See, for example, V E Buck, *Working Under Pressure*, Staples Press, 1972; also, E E Levitt, *The Psychology of Anxiety*, Paladin 1971, (First published by the Bobbs-Merrill, New York, 1967.)

2 See Chapter 9.

3 cf the concept of role-set; see R K Merton, 'The role-set: problems in sociological theory', *British Journal of Sociology*, Vol 8, No 2, June 1957, pp 106-20.

4 For a discussion of role ambiguity, see R L Kahn, D M Wolfe, R P Quinn, J D Snoek and R A Rosenthal, *Organizational Stress: Studies in Role Conflict and Ambiguity*, Wiley, New York, 1964.

5 For a systematic approach to the process of differentiation and integration, see P R Lawrence and J W Lorsch, *Organization and Environment: Managing Differentiation and Integration*, Harvard University Press, Cambridge, Mass., 1967.

6 For an interesting discussion of the role and personality of the integrator, see P R Lawrence and J W Lorsch, 'New management job: the integrator', *Harvard Business Review*, Vol 46, No 6, November - December 1967, pp 142-51.

7 M Dalton, 'Conflicts between staff and line managerial officers', *American Sociological Review*, Vol 15, 1950, pp 342-51.

8 See, for example, C Argyris, 'Today's problems with tomorrow's organizations', *Journal of Management Studies*, Vol 4, No 1, February 1967, pp 31-55.

9 See A W Gouldner, 'Cosmopolitans and locals: towards an analysis of latent social roles, I,II,' *Administrative Science Quarterly*, Vol 2, No 3, 1957-8, pp 281-306; No 4, 1957-8, pp 444-80; see also, R K Merton, 'Patterns of influence, local and cosmopolitan influentials', in R K Merton, *Social Theory and Social Structure*, Free Press of Glencoe, New York, 1949.

10 See J Morris and J G Burgoyne, *Developing Resourceful Managers*, Institute of Personnel Management, 1973, especially Chapter 3.

4

Stress and External Relationships: the 'Hidden Contract'

Dan Gowler and Karen Legge

Well before the recent upsurge in publicity for militant feminist movements such as 'women's lib', attention was being paid to the changing conceptions of marriage in our society.(1) Much of this interest centred around the relationship between husband and wife and, popularly, the picture was painted of married couples, partly through increased geographical mobility with consequent separation from kin and long-standing social networks, and partly through changes in social values, becoming more dependent on each other for support in the domestic sphere and enjoying a far closer emotional relationship than that known to their parents. Whereas their parents had a clearly defined division of labour into male tasks and female tasks, separate leisure pursuits and groups of friends, the 'modern' couple were seen increasingly to have a relationship in which many activities were undertaken together, with a minimum of task differentiation and separation of interests. Although these differences are mainly one of degree, the former type of relationship was termed a 'segregated conjugal role relationship', , and the latter a 'joint conjugal role relationship'.(2)

However, although it was hypothesized that, in the domestic situation, differentiation between the husband's and wife's activities was breaking down, an opposite trend, over a longer period, had been taking place in the relationship between their domestic and occupational roles.(3) In pre-industrial and early industrial society, the family had been the unit of both production and consumption (as in farming or cottage-industry communities), whereas, in modern society, with large-scale enterprise and complex division of labour, not only have the units of production and consumption become differentiated, but, more recently, the locations of production and consumption widely separated. Thus, where once the husband worked at home with his wife (admittedly on differentiated tasks, but with a high degree of mutual interdependence) now, typically, he not only works in a separate place (and at activities whose real nature his wife can often only guess) but one which may be miles away from his home and which may exercise little direct influence on the community in which he and his family live and consume. This is particularly true of the managerial classes who generally live in the outer suburbs of cities, further away from the centres of production than do the manual workers in the inner suburban or city areas (compare docking and mining communities with the 'commuter belt' in the home counties). This is a gross and highly debatable simplification of some trends in relationships between domestic and occupational roles, but this distinction does provide a point of departure for the examination of some of the stresses that confront the modern manager.

The trends outlined above may be expressed as in Figure 4.1, where we distinguish between occupational roles, in which individuals produce goods or services, and domestic roles, in which individuals consume the rewards of their productive roles. This relatively unusual definition of domestic roles creates some problems, particularly as to the role of the housewife, but this point is taken up later in the chapter. Figure 4.1 also distinguishes (for both occuptational and domestic roles) between a high and low level of conjugal role segregation.

Figure 4: 1 Aspects of the hidden contracts

	High conjugal role segregation	Low conjugal role segregation
Occupational/ productive roles	A eg Complete separation of occupational roles	B eg Shared occupational roles
Domestic/ consumer roles	C eg Complete separation of consumer-leisure roles	D eg Shared consumer-leisure roles

THE HIDDEN CONTRACT

We consider that, implicit in these trends and, indeed, sometimes explicitly stated between managers and their wives, lies a *'hidden contract'* on which organizations rely when assuming the conditions necessary for effective managerial performance and development. This 'contract' has several aspects, but we believe it useful to begin with the notion of a 'managerial career'. Although there has been much debate as to the validity of this concept,(4) managers are generally considered to have embarked on a career as opposed to a mere job. In other words, the occupational roles they hold are supposed to require a high degree of commitment on the part of the individual and to possess a continuous developmental character. The individual is said to develop a career by moving from one job or organization to another, continuously gathering and applying relevant experience for improved performance in a more senior position or in a more expert role of some kind.(5) This notion of a career is, in itself, a direct result of the trend towards the specialization of occupational roles expressed in Figure 4.1. A career, then, may be seen as a mechanism for coping with some of the individual and organizational problems that arise in the management of work organizations, particularly those concerned with task specialization, control and reward.

Looked at from the individual's point of view, a career does - as suggested above - imply 'commitment' to the maintenance and development of certain skills and qualities. Thus, 'commitment' may imply not only a long training prior to entering an occupation, but continuous training and study, often outside office hours; also, the willingness to take work home and to accept regular geographical mobility, possibly in return for promotion to more demanding and materially rewarding jobs. If an individual is career oriented, then the performance of his job may well absorb not only the bulk of his time, but much of his interest and aspirations - work may become the area in which he chooses to establish and develop his 'real' identity.

Now, if a manager accepts a career in these terms, this decision reverberates in his domestic life, for it is costly not only in terms of time and energy, but also in terms of his intellectual and emotional resources. Certainly it leaves him with reduced time and energy to devote to the daily running of the home. Furthermore, such research evidence as we have suggests that after returning from a hard day in the office, culminating in a commuter's journey home, the typical manager expects to find awaiting him a supportive, well-ordered domestic scene, where he can find rest and refreshment rather than another set of competing and demanding 'work' activities.(6) As one manager described his wife and home environment:

> I haven't gone far wrong with what I've got: she's always here when I come home and always willing to hear my moans. She makes me feel wanted.... She helps me to recharge after hectic days. Basically what I look for - home to me is **somewhere** where I can do what I please rather than what someone else pleases and my wife tolerates it; where one gets molly coddled to some extent - if one can put it that way.(7)

The hidden contract is not, however, based on conjugal role segregation in both the occupational *and* domestic spheres, though it may **seem** so at first sight. On the wife's side, the admission of the demands of her husband's career, and the provision of a well-serviced and supportive domestic environment, is in return for the development of a joint conjugal role relationship in other areas. Thus, for example, support for the husband's career aspirations is often on the understanding that there will be joint decision making on the allocation of the material rewards that result from his career progressions. Similarly, in the recognized 'free time' the husband has at the weekends and holidays, the wife expects a sharing of leisure pursuits, whether they are activities with herself, children or friends. In other words, her acceptance of the implications of this type of occupational role segregation in both their 'productive' lives is conditional on their joint participation in domestic and leisure activities that involve consumption. Put in terms of Figure 4.1, the main elements of the husband's and wife's occupational/productive roles are maintained in box A (high conjugal role segregation) *in return for* the maintenance of their domestic/consumer roles in box D (low conjugal role segregation). However, as we point out later, there is tension and stress involved in the relationship between boxes A and D.

Generally, this hidden contract functions in a satisfactory way for all the parties concerned, not least for the organization which is able to make heavy demands in terms of the manager's commitment and resources, on the assumption that a supportive back-up service awaits him at home. Yet the tensions embedded in this arrangement may lead to stresses strong enough to break, or substantially modify the hidden contract, with serious consequences for the organization in which the manager works, as well as for the two partners more immediately involved.

CHANGE, STRESS AND CONJUGAL ROLES

Elsewhere in this book we have defined 'stress' in situational terms, and related it to role theory.(8) Briefly, we argue that a situation becomes stressful when an individual feels unable to deal with the demands that his role places on him, yet when the rewards and punishments accompanying these demands make him wish to do so. In what ways then can the hidden contract become stressful to those involved?

For a start, there is the 'boundary' problem built into the hidden contract. Although the relationship between occupational/productive and domestic/consumer activities may be agreed in general terms, stresses may arise over the allocation of resources, in particular, of time and commitment to these two areas. Husband and wife may disagree, for example, as to how much of their resources should be devoted to the various spheres of activty - in other words, which should take priority and in which circumstances. A frequent issue here may be whether the organization demands 'too much' from the manager. A husband may consider that bringing work home every night, working weekends in emergencies, being prepared to be geographically mobile on request is a normal part of the career he desires, with both its material and intrinsic rewards. He may justify his heavy commitments to his occupational role in terms that it allows his family a materially rich pattern of consumption, even if he has little time or interest to participate in its enjoyment. As one manager, in a recent study, stated:

> It's inevitable that the higher up you move in business, the more incursion it makes into one's private life and I think wives find this hard to accept.... I don't think that I've neglected the family, I don't think it is neglect to the family.... This is something that women must recognize: that they have a fuller and more comfortable life as a result of this work. You can't have both, position, earnings, and a nine-to-five job.(9)

His wife though, clearly did not accept the weighting he placed on his occupational role, or his justification of allocating his resources in this way:

> His work has always come first, and we're pushed very much into the background.... When he comes home at night I have to listen to all the problems of the firm's activities, and when that's over, out come the books and papers and he works all night. I'm a bit sick of his industry... after all these years I've had enough of it.(10)

Latent stresses over the balancing of priorities and resources in the hidden contract frequently come to a head when a career crisis is reached, which may substantially affect one or both sides of the hidden contract. For example, stresses may occur over the geographical mobility involved in a manager's career. From the evidence we have (11) some wives, in fact, may welcome regular moves: there is the stimulation of meeting new people, seeing new places, having a new house to arrange, and generally breaking the monotony often associated with the housewife's role. In addition, as it is often associated with some promotion, a move may involve a perceived improvement in the pattern of consumption: more money, a better house in a 'nicer' neighbourhood, better educational opportunities for the children, etc. For such wives (and their husbands) a geographical move may, in fact, highlight the mutually beneficial working of the hidden contract.

However, for a great many wives, a move may be viewed as a highly stressful process. Not only is the husband, in the initial induction into his new job, likely to have occupational stresses to cope with and a heavier than usual demand on his time and other resources, but if the move involves promotion, increased responsibilities are likely to make this situation permanent. At the same time, partly because the husband is fully occupied with acclimatizing himself to a new occupational role, the wife is likely to bear the brunt of selling one house, finding, buying and arranging another, not to mention the settling of children into new play groups and schools, and generally establishing for the family a new, if loose, social network of acquaintances and contacts. As one manager put it:

> When you hear these couples talk it is obvious that when moving like this the wife's place is all-important. One's job tends to be all-embracing with only time at weekends, but the wife is faced with settling in with the house and place in town or village. If she is not prepared to smile or speak first, then you can remain silent within a community...(12)

This situation may be particularly stressful to the wife if she was firmly embedded in the previous community. Not only may the move have involved her in severing rewarding contacts in her local community (from which she may have sought to develop her own identity, separate from husband and children) but, if the family had been settled in the community for a number of years, she may have forgotten how, or lost confidence in her ability to establish and develop new contacts. Whereas for a husband a move may mean promotion, for a wife it may involve the loss of the status and identity she had acquired for herself in a local community, with the prospect of having to re-establish herself from scratch as the 'new girl'. Furthermore, when a manager enters a new job, formal procedures often exist to aid his induction, with his colleagues frequently taking the initiative; for his wife, formal procedures rarely exist to ease the process of establishing contacts. Generally, a successful induction rests on her own initiative and skill in developing informal situations.

A move may not only place stesses on each partner independently, but, at a time when the husband/manager particularly needs the benefits of his side of the hidden contract, the contract itself is most vulnerable. For while the husband may feel especially in need of a supportive domestic environment, his wife - coping with her own induction problems (and possibly those of their children) - may have neither the time nor inclination to give this support. In fact, she may well be seeking support herself, *via* an increase in their joint participation in 'productive' domestic tasks as well as in leisure-type activities. This may be particularly pronounced if the wife feels that she has been pushed into a move. Her view of the situation may be that, as her husband has got his reward of a new job, he 'owes it to her' - for her sacrifices - to make some compensation in the domestic sphere. Yet the husband, coping with the demands of the new job, may be unwilling or unable to do this. Furthermore, if the new job carries increased responsibilities and is generally more demanding, he may feel obliged to devote more time and other resources to his occupational role than previously, thus permanently shifting the balance of the hidden contract.

Although, at present, the hidden contract type of relationship between the manager and his wife, despite its potential stresses and strains, is the most common, there are signs that it is becoming less acceptable, certainly to the wives and in some respects to their husbands as well. In the study referred to throughout this chapter, it was found that a substantial number of wives in this type of relationship felt disquieted that they had little personal identity (apart from

husband and children).(13) This anxiety tended to
grow as their children became increasingly independent
and (which often coincided) the balance of the hidden
contract shifted in favour of the husband's occupational
role, as his seniority and responsibilities increased.
It was expressed in remarks such as:

> One of my problems in life is that I don't have any
> idea of what sort of person I am.(14)

> I've been married for twenty-three years now,
> during which time my husband's wishes, the house
> and... my daughter have always come first and I
> feel now that I want a life of my own.(15)

For most people, an obvious way to establish their
own identity is through a work role, yet housework
does not always fit the bill.* Not only is it
intimately tied up with developing and maintaining
other people's identities (eg in child rearing or the
supportive wife role), often at the expense of the
housewife's, but many of the activities comprise
routine maintenance on a highly repetitive cycle,
rather than developmental creative work. In the past
(and present, too) many manager's wives have been
happy to accept this occupational role, such as it is,
as their lack of training for a career disqualified
them from anything but a routine job. Given that,
for many managerial families, it has not been necessary
for the wife to work other than for its intrinsic
rewards, a routine job outside the house had provided

---

*This comment allows us to make the point that, in this
 analysis, we have treated the 'housewife' as an
 occupational/productive role. This raises two points.
 Firstly, in many of its 'productive' aspects the
 housewife's role is repetitive, arduous and unre-
 warding. Secondly, there is both an actual and
 conceptual confusion between housewife as producer
 and housewife as consumer. Moreover, this confusion
 has not only been a source of role conflict for the
 housewife, but also a source of conceptual difficulty
 for the academic researcher and commentator.

no substitute for a perhaps more varied and satisfying job within the house. Apart from this, few managerial husbands are eager to lend support to a wife taking a low-status job (which might even embarrass their own occupational status) that could take up time and energies 'better' spent on maintaining the supportive domestic environment.

This situation is, however, under pressure. Not only are changing social values supporting many women's desire to develop a more personal identity than that achieved through the roles of wife and mother, but structural changes are moving in the same direction. Not only are more women (including managers' wives) obtaining higher education and vocational training, but the rate of inflation and, in this country, new tax legislation encourage a wife to become income generating. Furthermore, the earlier age of marriage and child bearing, combined with reliable contraception and increased life expectancy, provide women not only with the opportunity to take training, after the child rearing years yet while still relatively young, but with a need for a career to fill the many remaining active years. In this case, other patterns of family life may well be developed at the expense of the type of relationship assumed in the hidden contract.

AN ALTERNATIVE PATTERN: 'DUAL-CAREER' FAMILIES

One such pattern, admittedly of a minority, is that of the 'dual-career' family.(16) It may be useful to consider it briefly, in contrast to the hidden contract form of marital relationship, for *it highlights in extreme form the stresses that may be imposed on the manager and his wife, if the wife herself takes on the same type of career commitment as her husband.* If both husband and wife have continuous (or near-continuous) careers, the hidden-contract type of relationship, by definition, is completely undermined. Although they may work at totally different jobs, the fact is that many decisions affecting one partner's career (eg about promotion that involves geographical mobility, or a heavier commitment in time and other resources) are likely to have repercussions on that of the other. In this sense, their occupational roles tend to be more competitive and less complementary than those of couples where the wife's occupational role is that of a housewife and where the hidden contract still operates effectively.

A major advantage of the hidden contract is that, for the husband pursuing a career, he is automatically provided with - and as of right - a comfortable supportive domestic environment. It is his wife's 'full-time job' to do so, and to mould this environment largely around the demands of her husband's occupational role. If both partners have careers, who is to provide the domestic supports that will encourage them and leave them free to realize their full career potential?

One solution, of course, is to buy in a 'wife substitute' who can at least tackle the routine aspects of running a home that are amenable to delegation. However, many of the back-up services that a wife normally provides, the dual-career family either cannot or would not wish to delegate, such as developmental, aspects of child care, or the building and maintenance of an adequate social network of acquaintances and friends. Further, if the system of delegation proves inadequate, too costly, or breaks down, the load is thrown back on both partners. Thus, whereas in the hidden contract form of marital relationship, stresses generally arise through one or both partners perceiving distortions in the allocation of resources to one or other side of the contract, in the dual-career family the stresses arise through the sheer overload of tasks and responsibilities that the partners carry. The emphasis is less on the allocation of the husband's and wife's respective resources, than on the fact that their joint resources are being overstretched. As one couple put it:

> It always seems to me as far as our own situation is concerned that it is tremendously dependent on

> good health; this husband and wife team, and the
> survival of the pair with individual work
> potential, is almost an energy thing... you do
> run out of steam.(17)

The way in which such families cope with the overload stress may in turn generate further stresses for both partners. The evidence we have (18) would suggest that when a couple is under conditions of strain, the domestic tasks will be reallocated in the direction of the more available partner. This may mean that a husband may find himself regularly having to tackle traditionally 'female' tasks (such as child care and cooking), and *vice versa*. Alternatively, husband and wife on occasion may be forced to neglect that, which under conditions of less strain, they would consider necessary obligations, eg attending their children's school functions, maintaining ties with close relations. In such circumstances, either partner may experience the dilemmas of personal identity especially as this may be reinforced by environmental sanctions, such as the disapproval for their pattern of life on the part of hidden-contract type families. Among the dual-career families, it has been reported that

> Issues as to whether the wife was being a good wife
> and mother, or more fundamentally a 'good human
> being' when she chose to pursue her career involve-
> ments, and whether the husband was sacrificing his
> 'manliness' in altering his domestic life to take
> on more of a participative role were widespread.(19)

Further, these overload and identity stresses, although consequent on both partners having a high career commitment, may ultimately feed back to initiate stresses in this area too. Because of the 'extra' domestic obligations, it is likely that both partners will be unable to give as much time to his/her career as those managers whose occupational roles are supported by the hidden contract. Also, it is likely that each partner's career on occasion may constrain the development of that of the other, eg promotion involving geographical mobility may not be acceptable to one partner owing to the lack of career opportunities there for the other. It may even happen that the wife may prove more successful at her own occupation than the husband at his and, consequently, face the choice of possible identity dilemmas for her husband, or the artifical curtailment of her own career development. Finally, Figure 4.1 suggests that other processes are likely to occur. For example, in the dual-career family the balance between productive and consumer roles (boxes A and D) might break down and partners go their own ways in their domestic/consumer roles, eg take separate holidays, live apart and so on, with both partners moving into box C, ie practising a high degree of domestic/consumer segregation. Alternatively, either of the partners may tailor his or her occupational behaviour to prevent this happening. In such a circumstance, we may say that this adjustment is in effect a move towards a lower level of occupational segregation, in which case the move has been from box A to box B. If this solution is adopted by one or other of the partners, there is likely to be a diminution in the level of occupational commitment in the cases concerned. The results of this might be lower levels of reward, both material and otherwise, and possibly serious conflicts with employers who may not welcome a lower level of occupational commitment, whatever the reasons.

The irony here is that stresses which arise from the dual-career family's choice to optimize on two careers rather than maximize on one would be largely alleviated if both partners could rely on the support and flexibility of action that is, say, open to the husband operating with the hidden contract. Small wonder then that, in spite of the stresses it contains, the hidden contract continues to survive and flourish, even if its days may be numbered.

CONCLUSIONS

In this chapter we have presented the view that one

source of managerial stress is to be found in the relationship between the manager's occupational and domestic roles. There is nothing new in this, but we have developed this theme in such a way as to incorporate the relationship between his wife's occupational and domestic roles. Furthermore, in both the case of the manager and his wife, we have equated the occupational role with the production of goods and/or services, and the domestic role with the consumption of the various rewards for the production of these goods and/or services.

We have also shown that, in many circumstances, certain assumptions about the wife's occupational role, ie her housewife role, are made by her manager/husband and by those who employ him. These assumptions often include the belief that there is and, indeed, should be a division of labour between husbands and wives, which result in a segregation of conjugal roles, with the wife providing a supportive, back-up service for her husband's work activities. We have termed this assumption the 'hidden contract', since the wife's supportive, back-up service is *assumed* in the contract of employment made between her husband/manager and his employer, but it is rarely *recognized* by either of these parties.

There is another aspect of this hidden contract, and we have pointed out that, in return for the acceptance and performance of segregated occupational roles, the manager/husband will share with his wife and family a large proportion of consumer decisions and activities. In other words, these segregated occupational roles are balanced or compensated for by integrated or less segregated consumer roles. However, it is reasonable to suggest that, while this aspect of the hidden contract is recognized and debated by managers and their wives, it is likely that employers do not accept its existence or importance.

We have also shown how both these aspects of the hidden contract break down in 'dual-career' families. Additionally, we have discussed the stresses generated by the erosion of the hidden contract, and the manner in which dual-career couples cope with this situation.

Finally, we have suggested that while the hidden contract is likely to survive, certain trends are beginning to undermine it. Furthermore, though not fully discussed here, these trends encompass female emancipation, increased divorce and separation, the increased cost of domestic services (which forces wives into paid employment while at the same time making it impossible to replace them at home), the changing status of children, and the strong value now being attached to the domestic/consumer roles, eg the contemporary emphasis on leisure and the quality of life.

All this suggests that employers cannot now assume that the hidden contract will always operate. Consequently, this question must become a matter for discussion, even though it will obviously be a difficult and sensitive topic. We advocate this not only to evade the conflicts that avoidance of the subject might perpetuate and accentuate, but also to encourage the discussion, design and implementation of arrangements which will enable both husbands and wives to develop their individual and joint potentials, whether in their occupational or consumer roles.

References

1   See, for example, E Bott, *Family and Social Network*, Tavistock, 1957; M Young and P Willmott, *Family and Kinship in East London*, Routledge and Kegan Paul, 1957; R Fletcher, *Family and Marriage in Britain*, revised edition, Penguin, 1966.

2   E Bott, ibid.

3   For a discussion of the changing economic functions of the family, see R Fletcher, op cit, pp 82-8.

4   J M and R E Pahl, *Managers and Their Wives*, Allen Lane, 1971, pp 17-34 and pp 78-107.

5 R and R Rapoport, *Dual-Career Families*, Penguin, 1971, p 18.

6 J M and R E Pahl, op cit.

7 ibid, p 260.

8 Especially Chapter 2.

9 J M and R E Pahl, op cit, p 216.

10 ibid, pp 216-7.

11 ibid, pp 61-7.

12 ibid, p 154.

13 ibid, p 111.

14 ibid, p 112.

15 ibid, p 216.

16 See M P Fogarty, R Rapoport and R N Rapoport, *Sex, Career and Family*, P E P and George Allen and Unwin, 1971; R and R Rapoport, op cit.

17 M P Fogarty, R Rapoport and R N Rapoport, ibid, p 343.

18 R O Blood and D M Wolfe, *Husbands and Wives: The Dynamics of Family Living*, Free Press of Glencoe and Collier-Macmillan, New York, 1960, pp 57-69; also, R and R Rapoport, op cit, passim.

19 R and R Rapoport, ibid, p 290-91.

PART 2
ROLES AND GROUPS

5

Leadership Style in Stressful and Non-Stressful Situations

Philip W Yetton

One of the major academic and applied management debates has been concerned with the question of participation in decision making: who should and how much? Traditionally, social psychologists have advocated participative management practices and condemned autocratic behaviour.(1) Their development of descriptive models based on individual differences is a direct consequence of such normative models. If it is good to be participative and bad to be autocratic, it would seem logical to measure how autocratic or participative a manager is and to construct descriptive models involving such measures. Questions such as 'does a manager use the same style to solve problems in high - and low-stress situations?' cannot be asked within such analytical frameworks. In this chapter a different framework is presented, in which such questions are, in fact, the *focus* of the analysis.

Recently, research has identified the need for contingency models of leadership behaviour,(2) in which behaviour is determined not only by characteristics of the individual but by the nature of the situation in which he finds himself. To some extent, Fiedler (3) follows in the tradition of the trait-based or individual-difference models, referred to above, rather than that of the new contingency models. He regards the manager's style as being fixed, and argues for the matching of the appropriate individual to each situation. In contrast, Heller, and Vroom and Yetton (4) argue that managers both *do* and *should* vary their styles as a function of the situation. In particular, Vroom and Yetton emphasize the stable patterns of a manager's behaviour and the heuristics with which he chooses a style to fit a situation. Their framework is used here to investigate how managers both should, and do, vary their behaviour as a function of changes in the level of stress inherent in the problems which they face.

An operational definition or measure of the stress that a typical manager feels in some decision making situation is beyond the scope of this chapter, and probably of its author. Instead, stress is treated as a situationally determined property and is measured in terms of the conflict between the manager and his subordinates and the conflict among his subordinates. High/high conflict situations (in which conflict between the manager and his subordinates is high, *and* conflict among his subordinates is high) are defined as high-stress situations, high/low and low/high problems as medium-stress situations, and low/low problems as low-stress ones. This construct of level of conflict *among* subordinates is the same as that used by Vroom and Yetton, while the construct of conflict *between* a manager and his subordinates maps directly onto their goal congruence construct. To distinguish these two types of conflict throughout the rest of this chapter, Vroom and Yetton's terminology of *conflict* (among subordinates) and *goal congruence* (between manager and subordinates) will be used.

Let us briefly consider the following two problems and the leadership style that two managers, David and Gordon, would use in each situation.

CASE A.

Recently, new machine tools have been installed on an engineering shopfloor, and the work patterns re-organized. Contrary to expectations, output has fallen and remained low. Labour turnover has increased and the morale of the workforce shows signs of deterioration.

Five first-line supervisors, one production engineer, and a supplies manager report to the section manager who is responsible for this shop. All the latter's subordinates were very keen to have the new equipment and are divided as to what has gone wrong. Their morale is still high, however, and they are anxious to correct the problem.

CASE B

The machine tools referred to in case A are presses, and the shop described makes aluminium and lead toothpaste tubes. It's Monday morning and it's the section manager's responsibility to draw up the week's production schedule. He has to decide, for example, how many lines will be working on aluminium and how many on lead, what size tubes should be produced and the length of the runs, and what provision needs to be made for breakdowns, given the week's demand for different tubes.

The first-line supervisors and supplies manager share the section manager's desire for a balanced schedule in which there are few short runs and in which the lead tubes, generally regarded as being difficult by the line operators, are equally shared across the 15 lines. There is rarely any strong disagreement over the make-up of the schedule, but it is important to get agreement on the priorities and procedures for revising the schedule in the event of certain lines breaking down. Without this prior agreement, there is likely to be some back-biting and fighting over which supervisor should take the bad jobs when another line has gone down.

Alternative Treatments

How might David and Gordon handle these problems? They might, on the basis of their knowledge of the situation, decide on the most likely cause of the first problem and draw up a new set of procedures to correct the situation. They might also simply lay out the schedule in the second case. On the other hand, before deciding on their solution, they might collect some information from their subordinates. Alternatively, they might call their subordinates into their offices individually, or as a group, and ask them for their ideas before making their decision. Finally, they might present the problems to their subordinates and attempt to reach agreement with them on the most appropriate solution to the problem. These are the five leadership styles identified by Vroom and Yetton and are presented in more detail in Figure 5.1.

Let us suppose for the moment that, in case A, David would talk to his subordinates individually before making the decision, while in the second case, he would discuss the problem with them as a group. On the other hand, Gordon would only collect some specific information from his subordinates before making the decision in case A, although he - like David - would discuss the second problem with his subordinates as a group before making the decision. How might such data be interpreted? While there is some suggestion that David may be slightly more participative than Gordon, the evidence seems to suggest that managers are more likely to be participative in case B than in case A. Although it is true that these two cases do vary in a number of respects, one way in which this difference might be accounted for is the differential level of stress

Figure 5:1 Alternative decision-making styles

S(1) The manager or leader perceives himself as solving the problem or making the decision himself, using information available to him at that time.

S(2) The manager or leader perceives himself as obtaining the necessary information from his subordinates, then deciding on the solution himself. He may or may not tell his subordinates what the problem is as he collects the information, but he perceives the roles played by his subordinates in the decision-making process as those of providing necessary facts or information rather than of generating or evaluating alternative solutions.

S(3) The manager or leader perceives himself as sharing the problem with the relevant subordinates individually, getting their ideas and suggestions without bringing them together as a group. He then makes the decision, which may or may not reflect his subordinates' influence.

S(4) The manager or leader perceives himself as sharing the problem with his subordinates as a group, collectively obtaining their ideas and suggestions. He then makes the decision himself, which may or may not reflect his subordinates' influence.

S(5) The manager or leader perceives himself as sharing the problem with his subordinates as a group. This group then generates and evaluates alternatives and attempts to reach agreement (consensus) on a solution. The manager perceives his role as much like that of a chairman. He does *not* try to influence the group to adopt 'his' solution, and he is willing to accept and implement any solution which has the support of the entire group.

(subordinates' conflict).

STRESS AND LEADERSHIP STYLE

By studying managers' behaviour across a large number of different problems, it is possible to establish whether David's and Gordon's participative shifts are, in fact, a function of the absence or presence of stress or simply due to some other factor. To examine this hypothesis, the behaviour of 72 managers over 30 cases was recorded, there being different levels of subordinates' conflict and managerial goal congruence. Each manager was asked to read the 30 cases and to indicate which of the five leadership styles from Figure 5.1 was closest to the style which he would adopt in such a situation.

Before presenting the results of this study, it might be useful to underline the difference between the traditional individual-centred models of leadership and the contingency model used here. In the traditional models, managers are described as autocratic or participative. Implicitly, it is assumed that - irrespective of the problem he is solving - any manager *uses* only one or two of the styles described in Figure 5.1 and that he *should* always be participative. The approach adopted here assumes that, as the problem changes, the style he uses changes, and that over a number of problems he *uses* and *should* use each of the five styles. The question we are concerned with is which style(s) does he tend to *use* in high, medium and low stress situations and which style(s) *should* he use.

Any comparison of behaviour for different types of problems would be greatly facilitated by assigning numerical values to the differing levels of participation represented by each of the five styles. The values adopted here are those presented by Vroom and Yetton, and reproduced in Figure 5.2. Discussions of the research from which these values were derived is beyond the scope of this chapter. However, the findings discussed later in this chapter are not, in fact, very sensitive to the values presented in Figure 5.2 so long as the rank order of the styles is preserved.

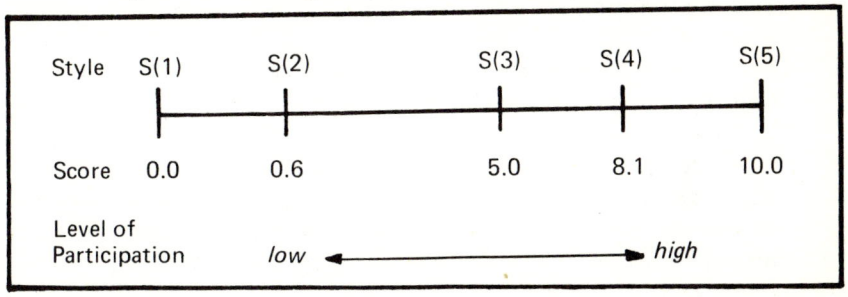

Figure 5:2 2 Managerial styles and levels of participation

Style	S(1)	S(2)	S(3)	S(4)	S(5)
Score	0.0	0.6	5.0	8.1	10.0

Level of Participation   low ←——————→ high

A statistical analysis of the data, using a two-way analysis of variance, reveals that differences in either goal congruence or conflict in isolation do not influence the typical manager's behaviour. However, the data do reveal that the combined influence of conflict and goal congruence has a powerful effect on his leadership style. He is more participative when goal congruence between himself and his subordinates is high and when conflict among his subordinates is low, than when either, or both, of the converses are true.

The behaviour is perhaps even more complex than this interaction suggests. A similar study of American managers(5) indicated that a further problem attribute moderates the impact of this interaction. It reports that managers are only more participative when, in addition to goal congruence being high and conflict being low, the acceptance of the decision by the subordinates is important for the implementation of that decision. Using the above scale, the average American manager was found to be 2.8 units more participative on problems in which he needs to develop his subordinates' acceptance of the decision to ensure its effective implementation than when he does not. Figure 5.3 presents the 72 British managers' average behaviour on the six problem types characterized by high/low goal congruence, high/low conflict, and high/low acceptance. Their participative shift is in the same direction and of similar magnitude (2.9 units). The findings from the two studies are consistent and can be expressed in the following proposition:

> The typical manager is more participative when acceptance of the solution by the subordinates is important, and stress is low (goal congruence between the manager and his subordinates is high, and conflict among subordinates is low) than when either or both of these features are absent from the situation.

One possible interpretation of this is as follows: when he needs to develop his subordinates' acceptance of a decision, the typical manager tends to be much more participative than when their acceptance is not critical. This participative shift is somewhat reduced in medium-and high-stress situations because some managers feel uncomfortable in, or unable to cope with, group decision processes in such situations. While this is only one possible explanation of the data, it is corroborated by a substantial amount of informal feedback obtained when discussing these findings with the managers involved.

So far, we have been talking about the typical manager's behaviour. It may be that different managers respond differently to the presence of stress. Let us reconsider David's and Gordon's behaviour. Initially, it was conjectured that David might be slightly more participative than Gordon. An alternative interpretation of the data might be that, in stressful situations (case A), David is more participative than Gordon, but that, in low-stress situations (case B), their behaviour is the same. This explanation would suggest that there is an interaction between individual characteristics and situational factors, ie a differential response to stress amongst managers.

Figure 5: 3 Interaction between stress and importance of acceptance

	IMPORTANCE OF ACCEPTANCE	
	high	*low*
Low stress (Conflict low, goal congruence high)	6.9	3.7
Medium stress (Conflict low, goal congruence low; Conflict high, goal congruence high)	4.0	3.1
High stress (Conflict high, goal congruence low)	4.6	4.0

Little research has been carried out within contingency frameworks such as the one presented here but even less work has been done on the interaction between a manager's individual characteristics and the situational factors. One of the few studies in this area (6) provides some information which indicates that these differential reactions do exist. In particular, that there is a group of managers who are very unwilling to use participative decision processes in medium-and high-stress situations while a slightly smaller group of managers strongly favour the use of group processes in such situations. The former group might be described as 'playing it cool' and keeping the protagonists apart. The latter, in contrast, are happy to deal with outbursts of hostility or conflict and believe in getting things out into the open and working them out, face to face, rather than sweeping them under the carpet in the hope that they will go away. It should be remembered that this paragraph is based on rather sparse and inadequate evidence. But, like the conclusions drawn earlier, it is supported by many managers' informal comments.

So far, we have attempted to describe what managers *do* in stressful situations. We now turn to what they *should* do. Vroom and Yetton propose seven rules which should govern a manager's choice of a leadership style in any situation. Two of these involve the dimension of stress as defined here, ie in terms of goal congruence and conflict.

Goal Congruence Rule

If the subordinates cannot be trusted to base their efforts to solve the problem on organizational rather than individual goals, S(1), S(2), S(3), S(4) should be used in preference to S(5). (See Fig 5.1) (An alternative which eliminates the leader's control over the final decision risks the quality of the decision being poor.)

Conflict Rule

If the acceptance of the decision by his subordinates is critical for its effective implementation, and they are likely to be in conflict, S(4) and S(5) should be used in preference to S(1), S(2) and S(3). The method used in solving the problem should enable those in disagreement to resolve their differences with full knowledge of the problem. Accordingly, S(4) and S(5) which provide an opportunity for those in conflict to resolve their differences in a face-to-face situation are preferred to S(1), S(2) and S(3) which do not facilitate such a resolution.

HOW THE RULES WORK: It should be noted that these rules assume that a manager has the necessary skills to manage a group decision in medium-and high-stress situations. It is possible that if he does not have the necessary interpersonal skills, one of the less preferred decision styles may lead to a better outcome than that from one of the prescribed styles.

Leaving aside this question of his ability to carry out a leadership style, how does the typical manager's behaviour compare with the behaviour prescribed by these two rules? The goal congruence rule implies that managers are slightly more autocratic when their subordinates' and their own goals are incompatible (high or medium stress) compared with situations in which the goals are compatible (medium or low stress). At first sight, this is consistent with the data in Figure 5.3. However, the rule advocates a shift from a feasible set of S(1), ..., S(5), from which the manager must choose on other grounds, to one of S(1), ..., S(4) as the situation changes from one of goal congruence to one of incongruence, whereas the behaviour reported in Figure 5.3 is primarily a shift from S(4) to S(3), ie from a group consultation process to an individual one. Thus, although managers tend to behave in the way that the goal congruence rule says they should, it would be difficult to argue that it actively *influenced* their behaviour. Rather, it can be argued that when faced with problems over which he is likely to encounter disagreement with his own views, he is unwilling to share the problem with his subordinates as a group. This is corroborated by the comment made by a number of managers that they were not willing to have their views attacked in public because this would weaken their authority.

The findings with respect to the conflict rule are rather different. This rule is frequently violated. In fact, managers seem to show a tendency to become more *autocratic* in the presence of conflict, whereas the rule suggests that they should be more *participative*.

Existing research provides little guidance as to why there should be so much conflict avoidance. One possible explanation lies in the fact that socialization processes in both Britain and the US do not develop skills in solving interpersonal conflict. As school children, we are likely, when caught fighting, to have been told to shake hands and make up. Furthermore, parents are likely to say that brothers and sisters like each other when, to any outside observer, it would appear that they detest the sight of each other. Conflict is 'resolved' in one instance by the exercise of authority, while in the other, its existence is denied. The average child receives little instruction in, or observes few examples of, the process of face-to-face inter personal conflict resolution. It would not therefore be surprising to find that avoidance is a typical response to stress situations. If this interpretation is correct, training in interpersonal skills would reduce the incidence of conflict avoidance and improve management decision making.

SUMMARY

In this chapter stress is seen as a property of the situation rather than as a subjectively experienced psychological state. Two properties of the problem - the level of goal congruence between the manager and his subordinates, and the level of conflict among his subordinates - are used to identify low, medium and high levels of stress situations. Low goal congruence and high conflict define high stress; low goal congruence and low conflict, and high goal congruence and high conflict define medium stress; and high goal congruence and low conflict, low stress.

Some evidence is given to suggest that the typical manager is more participative in situations of low stress than in those of medium or high stress. Two rules postulating how a manager should act in these different situations are then presented. A comparative analysis of the descriptive and normative models reveals a pattern of avoidance by the typical manager. It is conjectured that this reflects early socialization, in which the existence of conflict is either denied or resolved by the exercise of external authority rather than by means of a face-to-face interpersonal process, and the belief that public argument between a manager and his subordinates weakens the manager's authority.

References

1. R Blake and J S Mouton, *The Managerial Grid*, Gulf Publishing, Houston, 1964; R Likert, *The Human Organization*, McGraw-Hill, New York, 1967; D McGregor, *The Professional Manager*, McGraw-Hill, New York, 1967.

2. F E Fiedler, *A Theory of Leadership Effectiveness*, McGraw-Hill, New York, 1967; F A Heller, *Managerial Decision-Making*, Tavistock, 1971; V H Vroom and P W Yetton, *Leadership and Decision-Making*, University of Pittsburgh Press, Pittsburgh, 1973.

3. F E Fiedler, ibid.

4. F A Heller, op cit; V H Vroom and P W Yetton, op cit.

5. V H Vroom and P W Yetton, ibid.

6. P W Yetton, *Participation and Leadership Style: A Descriptive Model of a Manager's Choice of a Decision Process*, doctoral thesis, Carnegie-Mellon University, 1972.

6

Prerogatives, Participation and Managerial Stress

John Donaldson and Dan Gowler

The belief that greater participation by more people in decision making processes is both desirable and inevitable has received increasing support in recent years. In social and political life, various groups have challenged the decisions taken by powerful institutions, while worker participation in industry has been the subject of much discussion and some experimentation.

For many people, however, such developments are regarded as something of a mixed blessing, since they are likely to involve change, conflict and stress. Included in this category are a great number of managers, who have found that both the theory and practice of participation have enmeshed them in unfamiliar situations, where time-honoured prerogatives are challenged, discredited and in many cases abandoned altogether. Furthermore, for these managers, such situations have generated resentment, anger and often anxiety. It is this relationship between managerial prerogatives, participation and stress which provides the central theme of this chapter.

A 'SPECIAL CASE OF DELEGATION'

An interesting and useful approach to the relationship between managerial prerogatives, participation and stress is provided by McGregor, who sees participation as 'a special case of delegation', where the subordinate gains greater control, greater freedom of choice, with respect to his own responsibilities.(1) Furthermore, for McGregor, this participation through delegation is a legitimate means by which subordinates might be stimulated to accept their responsibilities, while improving their skills and abilities and increasing their job satisfaction, and so on. We have used the word 'legitimate' here, because McGregor sees this form of participation as neither a device for manipulating people nor an abdication of the manager's inalienable rights and duties.

Unfortunately, while McGregor's view has all the authority conveyed by such combinations of common sense and optimism, the advantages of delegation - whatever its forms or intent - are often more apparent than real. Moreover, it is often accompanied by misunderstandings, disagreement and anxiety. However, these rather negative comments require elaboration, since not only do we intend to question McGregor's opinion, but also to use a discussion of its basic assumptions as a point of departure for this chapter. Furthermore, we believe that many managers do, in fact, perceive participation as a form of delegation.

Firstly, delegation, in the generally accepted meaning of the word, does not necessarily involve participation, except in the minimal sense of taking part in an activity. For example, delegation is not always a completely voluntary act on the part of the delegator. For instance, a manager may feel forced to delegate certain duties to a subordinate when, under pressure of work, he is unable to perform them himself. On the other hand, in such a circumstance, the subordinate may have little or no say about the acceptability of the responsibilities so fortuitously presented to him. Indeed, he may find that he does not possess the experience, ability, or authority to undertake them.

The point we are making is that, for delegation to be participation, at least participation in the sense that it stimulates commitment, involvement and job satisfaction, a particular combination of factors has to pertain. In other words, this 'special case of delegation' appears to require special circumstances if it is to achieve positive outcomes such as greater understanding, tolerance and cooperation. In the following sections of this chapter, we consider the more negative aspects of delegation and participation, since these are some of the common causes of managerial stress.

FORMAL AND ACTUAL POWERS

The term delegation, whether or not used in reference to participation, implies that (a) a hierarchy of powers exists, among which is (b) the power to entrust these powers to others. Furthermore, in work organizations, these powers are vested in and, in fact, define a hierarchy of roles. It is these roles and powers which bestow those particular rights and duties that are sometimes termed 'managerial prerogatives'.

There is, however, another aspect to this, that *these formal powers are rarely coextensive with actual powers*, ie the ability to execute formal powers. This is not surprising, for if there is to be a complete match between formal and actual powers, the formal powers will not only have to be unambiguously defined, but will also have to encompass every unusual and unfamiliar circumstance, eg emergencies. Furthermore, those concerned have to accept that formal powers are legitimate however defined and whatever the circumstances. If this acceptance is not forthcoming, there is likely to be conflict, if and when attempts are made to use such powers.

It is both interesting and important to note, here, that mismatches between formal and actual powers are a frequent source of managerial tension and anxiety, since stress is likely to be generated in situations where managers believe they are unable to carry out their formal rights and duties. We return to this aspect of the relationship between managerial prerogatives and stress later in the chapter.

These comments do, however, create a difficulty in that they question the reality of the manager's formal powers. It is therefore useful to discuss this issue since, if these so-called formal powers are not matched by actual powers, the whole notion of managerial prerogatives, including the power to delegate, may be a mirage. Moreover, as commented above, the reality of these formal powers is related to aspects of managerial stress.

One way of approaching this question is to consider the current debate about the bureaucratic or pyramidal form of work organization. This is useful for, as commented above, the notion of managerial prerogatives assumes the existence of a hierarchy of roles and powers. However, to open the debate, there are those who maintain that, while many may believe that pyramidal, bureaucratic forms of work organization do and should exist, such social structures are either outmoded or not really operating in a hierarchical fashion at all. For example, there are researchers and commentators who have what might be called 'the world has changed' thesis. Thus, according to Bennis;

The bureaucratic 'machine model' was developed as a reaction against personal subjugation, nepotism, cruelty, and the capricious and subjective judgements which passed for managerial practices during the early days of the industrial revolution. Bureaucracy emerged out of the organization's need for order and precision and the workers' demands for impartial treatment. It was an organization ideally suited to the values and demands of the Victorian era. And just as bureaucracy emerged as a creative response to a radically new age, so today new organizational shapes are surfacing before our eyes.(2)

Bennis goes on to add that 'the conditions of our modern industrialized world are bringing about "the death of bureaucracy".'(3) These conditions include rapid change, growth in size, the complexity of modern technology, and changes in managerial behaviour and beliefs.(4) Bennis argues that these changes have made, or are making, the organizations based on a hierarchy of formal roles and powers expensive and inefficient anachronisms. Given these conditions, he argues for the recognition and/or introduction of more democratic, decentralized and participative forms of work organization.

All this is not to be taken to mean that hierarchies of formal roles and powers do not, or should not, exist. It seems to us that this is a matter of degree, and recent developments in thinking and research do in fact reflect a more pragmatic and contingent approach (5) to such questions. Researchers and practitioners are now beginning to ask questions such as 'In what circumstances do varying degrees of bureaucratization generate high organizational performance and individual job satisfaction?' For example, Morse and Lorsch(6) have carried out a comparative study in which they examined 'high performing' and 'low performing' organizations. (In each case, using management's own evaluation). They concluded that, for routine tasks, as in the automated manufacturing plants which they studied, highly formal relationships, rules and procedures were most appropriate. For creative, innovative tasks, as occurred in the research laboratories that they investigated, the converse was so. In other words, the 'high performing' manufacturing plant used the traditional, formal structure of relationships and controls, while the 'high performing' research laboratory used a participative style. The 'low performing' manufacturing plant used a participative style, and the 'low performing' research laboratory did not.

It is important to note that we have chosen this study not only as an example of the trend to a more contingent approach to such vexed questions as organizational design, but to illustrate the explicit and implicit tendency for managers and researchers to link participation with performance. The importance of this point, which is taken up again later, is that managerial beliefs about the nature of the relationship between participation and performance are likely to contribute to the arousal of anxiety and frustration.

AMBIGUITY AND ALIENATION

Given the situation outlined in the last section, it is not surprising that that contemporary managers often find themselves confused, alienated, angry, resentful and anxious. Firstly, there is the anxiety and resentment which stems from the actual erosion of formal roles and powers. As suggested above, the manager might find himself in the ambiguous situation where he (and others) expect his behaviour to conform to the notion that his formal powers are backed up by his actual powers. Naturally enough, if this is not so, one will probably find self-deception, high levels of anxiety, or the conflicts that arise when attempts are made to square the myth with the reality. Furthermore, it seems to us that attempts to introduce, say, management-worker participation in such circumstances may well result in the bizarre situation where managers try to share and delegate powers that they do not, in fact, possess.

Secondly, there is the form of alienation which stems from changes and/or contradictions in managerial values and beliefs about the nature of power and authority. For example, a manager might become alienated in the sense that he may believe that he is using illegimate means, eg an authoritarian managerial style, to achieve legitimate ends, eg high levels of output. Conversely, he may be alienated in the sense that he believes he is using legitimate means, eg a democratic, participative managerial style, which achieve illegitimate results, eg low productivity and high unit costs. In such circumstances, the manager may come to regard himself as some kind of deviant, which will probably be accompanied by stressful feelings of guilt and so on.

This form of alienation and anxiety is likely to be found in those situations where the managerial value system results in contradictory prescriptions. For example, where managers believe that they must improve, say, worker participation in decision making but where they also believe that they must give priority to production costs and schedules, delivery dates, standards of quality, profits, etc.

Another form of managerial stress will probably be found in those situations where differences exist between managers and their subordinates as to the form and/or consequences of participation. Put bluntly: subordinates may simply not wish to participate in anything. In these circumstances, managers may suffer feelings of irritation, guilt, inadequacy and anxiety, as their attempts to develop the various forms of participation are frustrated. They are certainly likely to feel very anxious in those situations where their superiors have indicated that they wish them to introduce participative activities, when their own subordinates have - for whatever reason - intimated that they have no intention of taking any part in the exercise.

Managers may, however, also suffer feelings of disappointment and confusion when a participative enterprise, where all may be involved and satisfied, results in no improvement in performance. To return to an issue raised earlier in this chapter, this disappointment and confusion may be compounded if the manager believes that, in all events, increased participation must result in higher performance. It is necessary to point out here that these comments are not to be taken to mean that we believe that participation is, in any absolute sense, antithetical to high performance; it depends on the circumstances.

PREROGATIVES, PARTICIPATION AND DEPRIVATION

Apart from the changes in structure, behaviour and values suggested by writers such as Bennis and Slater, (7) there is the very real problem that most of us - including most managers - have formed and reinforced our work-related attitudes and behaviours in hierarchical and bureaucratic organizations. We therefore find it difficult, if not impossible, to adjust to working in the more flexible, democratic and participative systems that many people now claim to be more appropriate to contemporary circumstances.

Argyris is very clear on this question of the causes and consequences of this form of conditioning; he writes

> ... the traditional pyramidal structure and managerial controls tend to place individuals and departments in constant interdepartmental warfare, where win-lose competition creates polarized stances, *that tend to get resolved by the superior making the decisions, thereby creating a dependence upon him.** Also there is a tendency towards con-

---

*Our italics. We stress this point because it represents another 'special case of delegation', ie *up* the hierarchial structure.

formity, mistrust, lack of risk-taking among the
peers that results in focusing upon individual
survival, requiring the seeking out of the scarce
rewards, identifying one's self with successful
venture (be a hero), and being careful to avoid
being blamed for or identified with failure,
thereby becoming a 'bum'. All these adaptive
behaviours tend to induce low interpersonal competence and can lead the organization, over the
long run, to become rigid, sticky, less innovative,
resulting in less than effective decisions with
even less internal commitment to the decisions on
the part of those involved.(8)

He is, however, relatively optimistic about these
difficulties, and comments that:

'One of the most promising strategies to induce
co-operation and integration of effort on crucial
business problems is the development of project
teams and the matrix organization.'(9)

Thus, Argyris looks to various forms of reorganization
to remedy the inadequacies of the more traditional
pyramidal structures, particularly those which might
generate free communication, risk taking, more
rational problem solving, and so on. In other words,
he not only recognizes that the hierarchical
pyramidal forms of work organization are becoming
less able to deal with the problems posed by
increasingly competitive and complex environments,
but that they have encouraged the development of
attitudes and behaviours which make the 'democrati-
zation' of them difficult and stressful. His
solution to this problem is planned organizational
change of the type indicated above, ie matrix
organization and project groups.

Argyris' comments, particularly those about 'the
seeking out of the scarce rewards', are of considerable importance when considering the relationship
between participation and managerial stress.
Furthermore, it is our opinion that it is this

relationship between rewards, participation and managerial stress which erects one of the most formidable barriers to the development of more democratic forms of work organization.

For one thing, given our society's emphasis on achievement, most managers expect to find a positive correlation between effort and reward. Thus, they expect higher effort to be matched by higher rewards. Secondly, most managers expect these higher rewards, whether tangible or intangible, to be linked in some way to the hierarchy of roles and powers. In other words, higher rewards are likely to be associated with a higher position in the organization. Thirdly, managers are also likely to perceive the powers or prerogatives vested in these positions as a reward in themselves. In short, managers will probably assume that these hierarchically ordered roles, prerogatives and rewards are closely related, if not indistinguishable. Fourthly, and a crucial point, if managers do believe that participation involves the delegation and/or sharing of their powers and prerogatives, they will probably also believe that it involves the delegation and/or sharing of their hard-earned rewards. Finally, such circumstances are likely to arouse in the managers concerned a sense of loss and deprivation. Consequently, any manager who feels this way is likely to view the prospect of increased participation in decision making with resentment or anxiety about the possible loss of status and/or rewards. Moreover, given these reactions, those involved may well resist the introduction of participative activities or, indeed, any form of innovation.

The sense of loss and deprivation described above is most likely to be experienced by those managers who believe that they occupy a 'fixed' position in the managerial hierarchy, eg supervisors. These managers might well view the introduction of any form of participation as an irreversible loss in status and reward. In other words, they will probably perceive the situation as a zero sum game. One consequence of this is that these first-line managers, whose commitment is vitally important to the success of any participative venture, are likely to react with active and/or passive forms of resistance. Active resistance might take the form of hostile criticism, while passive resistance might manifest itself in the infinite variety of ways available to the individual who just does not want to cooperate. For example, they might just opt out of the whole affair. The irony of this opting out is that the very activities which are supposed to stimulate social cohesion and collaboration result in the opposite state of affairs, eg social disintegration and avoidance behaviours. There is the final irony that this social disintegration and avoidance behaviour may also generate further anxiety, guilt, conflict and so on.

CONCLUSIONS

This chapter has attempted to show how managerial stress may be generated by the consideration and/or implementation of schemes aimed at increased participation in decision taking in work organizations. We have suggested, for example, that stress is related to inappropriate and confused ideas about managerial prerogatives. For example, that anxiety is raised when managers find that these prerogatives are limited or do not even exist. Furthermore, we have indicated that the stress generated by a perceived mismatch between a manager's formal and actual powers will be exacerbated if he also sees participation as a form of delegation. We have also discussed the point that the changing nature of contemporary work organizations is quite likely to increase confusion and bewilderment about these issues, with the result that those concerned experience the types of anxiety associated with ambiguity and alienation.

More specifically, we have considered the possibility that, in the light of technical, organizational and social changes, the entrenched attitudes and behaviours of managers, eg their ideas about managerial prerogatives, make it difficult for them to see the necessity for - let alone assist - the implementation of more participative styles of management and democratic forms of organization. We have discussed, too, the anxiety generated by conflicting values and misunderstandings about the presumed relationship between participation and performance.

Further, we have argued that, when managers, particularly those who perceive themselves to be 'fixed' in the 'lower' levels of the management structure, are confronted with involvement in more participative structures and activities, they are likely to experience a strong sense of loss and resentment.

These rather negative and somewhat pessimistic comments must not be taken to mean that we are in anyway against participation in decision taking, or anything else. Neither are they to be interpreted that we absolutely reject the notion that managers do or should have prerogatives or that managerial stress is always dysfunctional for the manager or the organization that employs him. They may, however, be regarded as cautionary tales, a reminder that this catalogue of ills might be visited upon those who take absolutist approaches to managerial problems in the belief, for instance, that participation, whatever its form, is good/bad and desirable/undesirable, whatever the circumstances.

The lesson that we draw is that managers might take a closer look at the powers they think they possess and the changing nature of the organizations in which they work. Managers might also approach the introduction of any new idea in a contingent manner, be it a technical or a social innovation. We believe that this more realistic and, admittedly, pragmatic stance would avoid the forms of managerial stress generated by attempts to do the 'right' thing in the 'wrong' situation; participation is no exception to this rule.

Finally, we believe that a sympathetic understanding of the manager's difficulties, particularly those that arouse feelings of deprivation, frustration and anxiety, will prevent the harsh and unrealistic judgements that sometimes accompany the more mechanistic forms of management appraisal.

References

1   D McGregor, *The Human Side of Enterprise*, McGraw-Hill, New York, 1960, p 130.

2   W G Bennis, 'Beyond bureaucracy' in W G Bennis and P E Slater, *The Temporary Society*, Harper and Row, New York, 1968, p 55.

3   ibid, p 55.

4   ibid, pp 55-6.

5   For an introduction to contingency theory, see P R Lawrence and J W Lorsch, *Organization and Environment: Managing Differentation and Integration*, Harvard University Press, Cambridge, Mass., 1967, Chp VIII, pp 185-210 For practical examples of contingency or best-fit approaches to such problems as the selection of a wage payment system or the improvement of job satisfaction, see T Lupton and D Gowler, 'Selecting a Wage Payment System', *Research Paper No 3*, Engineering Employers' Federation, 1969, and E Mumford, *Job Satisfaction, A Study of Computer Specialists*, Longman, 1972.

6   J J Morse and J W Lorsch, 'Beyond theory Y', *Harvard Business Review*, Vol 48, No 3, May/June 1970, pp 61-8.

7   W G Bennis and P E Slater, op cit.

8   C Argyris, 'Today's problems with tomorrow's organizations', *The Journal of Management Studies*, Vol 4, No 1, February 1967, p 32.

9   ibid, p 32.

7

Stress, Uncertainty and Innovation:
some examples from the installation of large—scale computer systems

Enid Mumford

THE PROBLEM

Working in very uncertain situations leads to stress. Such situations are characterized by an absence of specific and relevant information, and months, or years, may elapse before the correctness of decisions and actions is apparent. There is also a lack of knowledge concerning cause and effect, and people cannot clearly perceive the consequences of the decisions and actions which they are taking.(1)

Situations of this kind are associated with the introduction of large-scale innovation, such as major computer systems, which have particular uncertainties associated with them. The design phase frequently takes place in an environment which is technologically dynamic, with new, improved methods for problem solving that result from developments in hardware, software and peripheral equipment. Planning and implementation necessarily embrace a large variety of technical, social and economic factors, many of which may be overlooked until they are forced to management's attention by some danger signal.

Managers are increasingly having to cope with this form of innovation, although they may have little previous experience of either computer technology or large-scale change. In coping with it, they have to form relationships with the relevant technical experts - the computer specialists - and are subject to pressure from top management for fast and successful results. The achievement of a collaborative and helpful relationship between top management, computer specialists and user-department management* is not easy, and it is useful to begin by considering the role of each group in the change process.

Top management generally assume one of two roles. Sometimes, they see computer developments as part of strategic planning and play a major policy-making role; at the other extreme, decision making on computer utilization is left to specialists, and top management merely sanction these decisions and provide the necessary finance. In either role, their rather remote position is a shield against uncertainty-induced stress, though not against risk.

Computer specialists have the stress of meeting targets and deadlines but usually have the certainty of controlling the design process and of having technical competence. This last fact may affect the extent to which computer innovation takes place in a firm. Knight,(3) in a study of the computing industry, found that firms which innovated had people with both a detailed understanding of the problem to be solved

―――――――――――――――――――――――――――――――――――――

*The line management in those departments where computer-based solutions are to be introduced, and who take direct responsibility for the successful implementation and operation of new EDP systems.(2)

and a knowledge of the specific technology that led to each particular development.

User management is the group with the greatest amount of uncertainty and therefore in the greatest potential stress situation. Managers have to play a major part in implementing the new system and will be held responsible for its successful operation. The extent to which they define their own role in the change process, or allow others to define their role for them, will have a major effect on the amount of stress which they feel. It is the problems of user management on which we shall concentrate in this chapter.

THE RISKS OF COMPUTER INNOVATION

Computer innovation, because it is still comparatively new, yet developing rapidly, seems a particularly risky form of innovation. As risk situations can easily turn into stress situations, it is important to analyse the nature of the risks associated with the introduction of computer systems.

Financial

A large-scale computer system may cost several million pounds and require considerable benefits to offset this cost.

Operational

If the system is novel, designed to tackle an entirely new problem, or an old problem in a new way, then it may not have been rigorously tested operationally. In these circumstances, the user manager's question will always be, 'Will the system work'? He may fear that if it fails, the computer manufacturer or even his own management services department may try very hard to demonstrate that the fault is his, not theirs.

Human relations

Computer innovation, like all change, has human consequences. The new system may fundamentally alter the skill structure and staff levels of the manager's department. Such changes, if not handled skilfully, are potentially dangerous in industrial relations terms.

Political

Major technical change usually implies the reallocation of scarce resources, a process in which some groups gain and others lose. Resources may be material items, such as equipment, but they may also be money, skills or services, all of which give the holder status and sometimes power. Major change is characterized by groups attempting to gain additional status, power and influence through the acquisition of more resources and by other groups attempting to retain what they already possess.

Thus, with major systems innovation, the relationship between systems designers and users frequently has strong political elements, with users perceiving the systems group as a threat, as when the user manager thinks that his knowledge and expertise are no longer relevant in the new technical situation, and fears that he will thus lose autonomy.

Environmental

In the context of innovation, the firm's external environment is also a risk factor. If it is stable and the firm is economically sound, the consequences of a technical mistake will be less serious than if the firm has to respond to new external constraints while under financial pressure.

Today, organizations exist in complicated and rapidly changing technical and market environments.(4) They are confronted with the problem of economic factors being interrelated with technical, human and political factors, and presenting a shifting complex of pressures to which managers have to respond,(5) especially when introducing large-scale technical change. If planning processes do not take account of these problems, obsolete and irrelevant plans will be implemented.

It is not surprising, then, that both computer specialists and user management are nervous of the economic consequences of failure, or of only limited success, especially if environmental, technical or human constraints mean that plans cannot be easily modified.

SOURCES OF MANAGERIAL STRESS

Risk situations are potentially stressful because high financial losses can be incurred if the wrong decisions are taken. But the processes of change generate their own stresses, and the user manager has to cope with these.

The Problem of Role

McKinsey has stated that an important factor in the success of new computer systems is their operational 'feasibility'.(6) That is, will they be used by, and acceptable to the management and staff who receive them? This acceptability seems often to be related to the extent to which user departments are able to participate in decision processes concerning the proposed installation. The role played by a user manager in the change process can vary dramatically. If he is knowledgeable about computer systems, can identify his own problems and appreciate which of these best lend themselves to a computer-based solution, he will ask the computer specialists for assistance in solving his problems, evaluate their proposals in terms of his needs, participate in the design of the new system and take responsibility for its implementation and operation. This kind of active, participating manager seems rather rare.

More frequently, one encounters the passive manager - usually so because of his lack of knowledge and competence in this new technical area. He plays little part in planning and designing the new work system, which he implements with doubts, qualms and reluctance. Such a manager is likely to experience high levels of stress, since he is not in control of his own situation, yet is likely to be held responsible for the successful operation of the new system.

In some situations, this passive role is thrust upon the user manager by a more powerful computer specialist group. He has no alternative, for the computer group does not invite him to participate in their decision processes and he lacks the power and knowledge to insist on involvement. Computer specialists differ considerably in their approach to user management. Some see themselves in a service role and wait until line managers approach them with problems, while others are more actively engaged in seeking out problems and believe that a major function is to develop more innovative attitudes and interests in line managers and their problems. The latter approach is more stressful to the line manager, as he is likely to have change thrust upon him. The author has come across situations where the computer department has adopted this 'ginger' role yet, at the same time, refused to accept 'managerial' responsibility for systems design and implementation. This is a situation of considerable stress. The user manager is forced into the non-viable role of a controlling position without the knowledge and competence to exercise control. An important factor in the easy assimilation of new computer systems is an early agreement between computer specialists and user management on a sharing out of responsibilities, assigned on the basis of experience and competence.

When a department has not previously associated with computer specialists or when this kind of technical group is new to a firm, the situation will be fraught with uncertainty for the manager because he will not know what can be legitimately expected from them. A process of bargaining for areas of responsibility in the change process will take place, clouded by a lack of understanding of the nature of the tasks available for allocation. There is likely to be a great deal of assuming, dropping and transferring of task responsibilities as each group attempts to define its activites in terms of its competence, needs and objectives. Kahn *et al* point out that when this process of allocation is difficult to resolve, conflict is liable to break out between the groups.(7) Some managers will react to this with aggression and attempt to stake their claims forcibly, others will seek to protect themselves from a stressful situation by trying to withdraw and leave others to take the decisions.

If the manager of the user department is under stress because he feels that he is not in control, his department is also likely to be fearful and anxious. Melman has pointed out that ultimate power always resides at the bottom of any hierarchy because it is this group which, in the long term, has to operate the new work system.(8) This may mean that the new computer system never goes into really efficient operation because neither manager nor staff want it.

The Problem of Knowledge

It is suggested above that an active, controlling role places a manager under less stress than a passive, recipient role and that an important reason for a manager assuming, or accepting, a passive role is an absence of knowledge resulting in a lack of competence to cope with a novel problem. This places a number of different stresses on the manager. Because he is not involved in the design of the new system, he is likely to be worried that - not understanding the end-product - he will have great difficulty in running his reorganized department. In the words of one user manager,

> If anything went wrong in the office before the new computer system was introduced, I was able to go out there and put things right on the basis of my 25 years' experience with the work. Now if anything goes wrong I stay out of the way because I don't know enough about the new computer system to be able to cope.

Further, the manager is required to act as a change agent, to transform the technical state of his department, a process which usually involves a major reorganization of work procedures and is itself both skilled and difficult. The user manager is likely to experience pressure from top management to get the new system operational and efficient as soon as possible, as the latter is looking for a return on its investment. Yet successful assimilation of technical change involves the development of new attitudes and skills in the group using the new system and it will be the manager's responsibility to ensure that his staff acquire these. To achieve success, he will need to be a good diagnostician of the human problems associated with the change process and an excellent communicator to his staff. Many managers will have difficulty in these areas and will be under stress because they can meet neither the expectations of top management nor those of their own staff. The new work system operates at low efficiency because staff are inadequately trained, and discontented and anxious because they cannot cope easily with the new methods of work.

The Problem of Acceptability

A further personnel problem for the manager is his uncertainty about how his subordinates will react to the introduction of the new system. Most computer systems make users afraid of possible redundancy, whether these fears are valid or not. Thus, many staff will leave the firm altogether or seek transfers to other departments not scheduled for change, and so create considerable difficulties for the manager. At a time when he is extremely vulnerable and urgently requires labour stability in his department, some of his most valued and experienced staff may leave. If the computer is leading to staff savings this movement certainly helps to reduce staff numbers, but the manager may find that he has lost his most valuable staff and is left with the newest and least experienced ones. Stress also occurs when a computer system is introduced with the objective of achieving staff savings, as this places the manager in a conflict situation between the goals of top management and the job security needs of his subordinates.

The Problem of Reconciling Different Interests

Complex innovative decisions are taken by groups rather than individuals. These groups are unlikely to have a complete identity of interest; rather, they may have major conflicts of interest which have to be recognized and reconciled during the change process. Such conflicts and the differential distribution of power and influence within a decision taking and implementation group will cause stress for the user manager. Technical specialists tend to have different interests from those of most line managers. Eagerness to optimize a technical potential, often leads them to design systems which have high technical competence but largely ignore human needs, such as a desire for job satisfaction. The average computer man is not trained to take such factors into account.

Armed with advanced technical knowledge, the 'expert' has a degree of power over user managers since they cannot challenge him in this area and, hence, may be forced into a dependency relationship. To combat this 'expert' power, the user manager has to generate support for his own alternative demands. Invariably, it has to be sought from top management and can only be achieved by undermining the 'expert's' proposals. The user manager may be able to demonstrate to top management that the technical aspects of the proposed change are less significant than the business of human relations aspects and that these have been inadequately considered. Although this strategy may be necessary for the survival of the manager in his job, it will surely lead to a conflict situation in which there is considerable divergence of interest between the technical specialist and the user manager. This situation is common with most innovative decisions, but eventually conflict has to be reconciled and areas of mutual interest identified.

This eventual reconciliation of interests will be easier if the technical expert interprets his role as a facilitator of change rather than simply as an agent of high-level technology. Being a facilitator implies recognition of the human relations factors in the change situation and a willingness to abandon some technical goals in order to achieve human goals. Career history appears to figure in this role interpretation. If the computer specialist is a long-service employee, recruited into the computer department from less technical areas of the firm, he is likely to be indoctrinated into company values and to be conscious of the non-technical needs of the user department. If, however, he has always been a technical man, he is likely to define his job in purely technical terms and be unable to take account of human factors. He may have difficulty in understanding the user manager's concern for human relations and departmental morale, or even the very real business constraints under which the latter may have to operate.

A narrowly defined role and set of responsibilities reduce the computer specialist's stress and uncertainty by limiting the number of variables of which he has to take account. But it is likely to increase the uncertainty of the user manager, who may believe that his personal and departmental interests are being overlooked and that the computer specialist is more interested in the technical efficiency of his system than in the human needs of the user situation.

CONFLICTS OF INTEREST AND POLITICAL BEHAVIOUR AS SOURCES OF STRESS

Because major innovation causes major change, one potential source of conflict is the fact that some participants in the change process will hope to achieve advantages, while others will see themselves as losing past gains. A successful reconciliation of these interests requires compromise, which may mean that the technical specialist has to relinquish some potential technological gains, while the user manager has to reconcile himself to unwelcome aspects of change.

Many of the interests which have to be reconciled are organizational rather than personal. The computer specialist may believe that an optimal technical solution would lead to greater organizational efficiency, while the user manager may feel that permitting technical objectives to override human goals will affect the well-being of his customers and/or the morale of his staff. But both the computer specialists and the user manager are also likely to have a need for influence, status and perhaps even job security, and a part of their evaluation of the proposed system will be its likely effect on these personal interests. Their position in the company's power hierarchy will affect the extent to which they can successfully pursue these interests, since it will determine the amount of pressure for support that they can exert on other powerful groups or individuals. All this political activity is likely to be stressful to the user manager. He is likely to feel unprotected, and therefore subject to more stress, because he does not have the information, skills and knowledge of the technical specialists, and thus finds it difficult both to contest their point of view and to rally the support of other managers in steering the proposed innovation in a direction that assists his interests.

Pettigrew(9) has recently documented this political element, suggesting that joint decision making activities between specialist and operational groups are more likely to be characterized by bargaining than problem solving; he quotes Lynton that such bargaining is likely to include the careful rationing and deliberate distortion of information; rigid, formal, circumscribed relations; suspicion, hostility and disassociation.

Pettigrew convincingly demonstrates the dominant political element in decision making for major innovation. He sees this process as involving a contest over scarce resources, with both specialists and managers seeking to use the decision making situation to further their own interests and to secure more influence and control within the organization. Innovation generates uncertainty and causes stress for the user manager because it has the potential to alter existing patterns of resource sharing. New resources may be created by the innovation and come within the jurisdiction of a department, group or individual who have not previously had this kind of resource, and who may then perceive these resources as an opportunity for gaining status and power relative to others in the organization. At the same time, those who see their interests as being threatened by the proposed change may resist such allocation of new resources. In this way, stress is generated as a result of political behaviour.

Pettigrew suggests that, in any major innovation involving managers and technical experts, many of the resulting stress issues are related to the claims which each side makes for its knowledge and skills to be regarded as important resources. The computer specialist may argue that there must be increased recognition of the value of technical information as a business resource; the user manager, that his knowledge of the customer market and business experience is of greater value. He may also fear that if the claim of the computer specialist is recognized by top management this may lead to his own skills and competences being undervalued so that

he loses status and influence within the organization.
One of the reasons for disappointed expectations with
computer systems is because of the overselling which
many computer specialists adopt to get their preferred solution accepted by the user department.

Pettigrew adds that an undue emphasis on political
considerations may be a feature of major innovative
decisions simply because it is extremely difficult to
predict with any accuracy the consequences of one
technical choice against another, or even to recognize
a satisfactory solution. This leaves a large element
of subjectivity in the final choice, and scope for
battle between computer specialists and user managers,
as each pushes for the solution which they believe
to meet their own interests best.

COPING WITH THE STRESS OF INNOVATION

Major innovations are expensive and difficult to
change, which means that failure or partial success
will have to be lived with for a long time. Yet
because they are innovations, there may be little
available experience on the best solutions for
particular problems and situations. This is
particularly true of computer systems, which are
still quite new in many firms and also extremely
expensive. The major risk of failure through an
unsuccessful system design is taken by the computer
specialist but the successful operation of that
system is the responsibility of the user manager, and
he may be held accountable for poor operation which
is, in fact, due to poor design. Some computer-
system designers have been known to pass the blame
for defective systems on to the user manager in an
effort to avoid having to accept responsibility
themselves.

How can the manager cope with this kind of
situation? First of all, *knowledge* is his greatest
safeguard. If he understands the operating requirements of the new system and ensures that his staff

are fully trained before its introduction, he is able to withstand criticism from either computer specialists or top management. He can show where the failures really lie, and avoid the stress of accepting blame for factors outside his own control. An even better situation is where the user manager has sufficient knowledge to participate in a cooperative problem solving approach with top management and computer specialists. In this situation, there are likely to be *supportive values* and a tolerance of the inevitable mistakes that accompany major innovation: an important condition in the avoidance of stress.

Information can also help the manager to avoid stress. Innovation produces much uncertainty because crises can erupt apparently without warning, not because signals do not exist, but because they go unnoticed. Good *monitoring, feedback* and *rectification* systems are therefore excellent aids for avoiding stress. The computer specialists are likely to assume responsibility for monitoring the technical aspect of the new system, but even higher costs may be incurred if something goes wrong with the human part of the system, leading to strikes, increased absenteeism or labour turnover. The manager who wishes to avoid the stress of such a crisis will monitor his staff's morale so that he can take fast, remedial action as human relations problems occur.

The manager must also recognize that the situation into which the new system is being introduced is not static. His staff, or his customers, may be developing new attitudes and needs while the change process is taking place; furthermore, many of these may be created by it. Any innovation plans must therefore be adaptive to these environmental changes. Beer suggests that plans for problem solving, constructed at one moment in time and implemented unaltered at a later date, will surely be inappropriate because of inadequate responsiveness.(10)

Effective monitoring of internal and external environments will help to avoid this problem. This monitoring is a difficult undertaking requiring the manager both to observe and respond to changes in his own situation. If he does not do this, he may experience stress and uncertainty because actions that he is taking will not fit the current needs. Nevertheless, all factors in the change situation are not potential stress generators. A feature of novel innovation which will in fact prevent stress is *ignorance*. A lack of experience can hinder the manager or his top management from identifying when poor decisions have been made and inferior work systems implemented. Everyone may be happy with the new system because it is superior to the old manual system, not appreciating that other solutions would have been both cheaper and more efficient. In this situation, 'ignorance is bliss' and is an aid to the avoidance of stress. Also, the time span between the design and eventual implementation of a computer system may be very long. Early objectives may be forgotten as time passes and so there may be no rigorous post-change evaluation to establish whether they have been achieved.

Internal Politics

Politics are a part of organizational life, and this needs to be recognized if stress is to be avoided. Political factors can never be removed from any change situation but their dysfunctions can be reduced through the establishment of effective mechanisms such as *good communication* and *consultation* for the reconciliation of different interests, through bringing them into the open and allowing negotiations to take place. Unhappily, it usually requires good relationships for this to materialize. Too often, the political factors - though greatly affecting the decisions being taken - are not openly discussed. Groups seeking to gain power and influence from the change process may deliberately try to ensure that they are *not* discussed, since such groups want a solution that furthers their interests and not the kind of compromise solution that results from negotiation. Organizations in which mechanisms for consultation already exist, such as the Civil Service, are at an advantage in times of change, as everyone is accustomed to communicate and consult. Private industry which seeks to do this to facilitate change may find that a considerable learning period is required before these mechanisms begin to function effectively.

Another strategy that helps to avoid the dysfunctional aspects of internal politics is the agreed allocation of responsibility for different aspects of the change, to different groups. During a time of major change, both computer specialists and user management are prone to suffer from role strain and role uncertainty because neither they, nor the groups with whom they interact, understand precisely what their particular skills are, and how best to use them. Because they have not thought through the nature of the specialist role in a meaningful way, top management may not clearly inform its computer specialists which tasks they are to perform. Hence, they may try to usurp aspects of the change process which the user manager regards as being within his own jurisdiction and which he is reluctant to relinquish. Again the user managers, unaccustomed to computer specialists, may be unclear about where their responsibilities lie. Situations in which the computer specialists are defining their role differently from the user manager will certainly cause stress, and there is likely to be considerable negotiation before task allocation is successfully completed. If unsuccessful, the user manager will have to reconcile himself to a perceived usurpation of his functions. A lack of confidence between both groups will influence the kind of interpretations which each makes about the behaviour of the other. Whereas a computer group may see itself as innovative, creative and rational, user management may see them as having the opposite tendencies.

CONCLUSIONS

No management job will ever be completely free of stress; in fact, this could be dysfunctional for the organization and for the manager's personal growth and development. Nevertheless, stress is likely to increase at certain times and to be intensified in certain roles. In this chapter, computer innovation and the role of the user manager have been selected as examples of stress situations and stress roles, but many other activities generate uncertainty, and stress may be intensively experienced by people responsible for coping with this uncertainty. The degree to which stress *is* experienced is to some extent a function of role and personality; it is also related to knowledge and experience. For a manager presented with the problems of major change, the best protection from stress is a knowledge of the difficulties likely to occur, an ability to perceive which of these are present in his own situation, and the influence and skill to manipulate the change situation in such a way that his department's and his own interests are protected. A collaborative situation in which a problem solving group of experts and users jointly tackles the change situation is helpful in reconciling different interests and spreading the 'stress load'. Good advice to the manager in a stress situation can be found in the words of a Chinese philosopher,

> Before it move, hold it
> Before it go wrong, mould it
> Drain off water in winter before it freeze
> Before weeds grow, sow them to the breeze.
> You can deal with what has not happened, can foresee
> Harmful events and not allow them to be.

References

1   P R Lawrence and J W Lorsch, *Organization and Environment: Managing Differentiation and Integration,* Harvard University Press, Cambridge, Mass., 1967.

2   E Mumford, *Job Satisfaction, A Study of Computer Specialists*, Longman, 1972.

3. K E Knight, 'A descriptive model of the intra-firm innovation process', *Journal of Business*, Vol 40, No 4, October 1967, pp 478-96.

4   H A Simon, 'Rational choice and the structure of the environment', *Psychological Review*, Vol 63, No 2, March 1956, pp 129-39.

5   F E Emery and E L Trist, 'The causal texture of organizational environments', *Human Relations*, Vol 18, No 1, February 1965, pp 21-32.

6   McKinsey Associates, 'Unlocking the computer's profit potential', *McKinsey Quarterly*, Vol 5, No 2, 1968.

7   R L Kahn, D M Wolfe, R P Quinn, J D Snoek and R A Rosenthal, *Organizational Stress, Studies in Role Conflict and Ambiguity*, Wiley, New York, 1964.

8   S Melman, *Decision-making and Productivity*, Wiley, New York, 1958.

9   A Pettigrew, *The Politics of Organizational Decision-making*, Tavistock, 1973.

10 S Beer, *Decision and Control*, Wiley, New York, 1966.

8

Stress in the Management of Change

Allan Warmington

This chapter describes the environment in which the management of a change programme is likely to be set up, and analyses the sources of stress which are inherent in the situation. The analysis owes a great deal to the writer's own association with, and observation of, a group of managers engaged in a successful change programme,* but the focus will be on the general problem of stress in this context, rather than on events and reactions in one particular programme. Organizations show marked differences in

---

*I must acknowledge gratefully the amount this paper owes to the ideas discussed by my colleagues on the company change team concerned, with whom I have been working over the least four years, and to whom some of the problems discussed are only too familiar.

structure and patterns of relationships, and the circumstances in which change programmes are established differ greatly from one company to another. The manifestation of these stresses and their relative importance therefore varies also. Nevertheless, certain general characteristics are likely to be present in any programme.

The management of planned organizational change and improvement has recently emerged as a recognized specialism in a few large industrial firms. 'Planned change' usually means the creation of a specialist group of managers charged with effecting changes in organizational structure, management style, patterns of relationships or decision making processes.(1) Change is rarely desired for its own sake. There may be a recognition that the organization faces a changed situation - a change in product or resource markets, a change in the techniques being employed by the company itself, or by its competitors - and that it must be made more adaptable. Alternatively, those managing the organization may wish to induce changes in style or structure, with some idea that they will lead to improved performance or soon become necessary because of expected environmental developments, or because they will be looked for by employees or society at large. Change may be planned as a means of overcoming stresses which are already apparent, or it may be a move to prevent those stresses developing and to enable the organization to meet and be prepared for new circumstances when they arise.

The management of change of this kind has certain essential characteristics,(2) and our contention is that these are the source of a number of different manifestations of stress. The most obvious kind is likely to be experienced in the form of difficulties between members of the change programme and the people in the rest of the organization, whom it is their main task to influence; these may be difficulties of communication, of the perceived legitimacy and acceptability of the programme, or difficulties due to natural resistance by those who feel that they are under pressure to change their behaviour. Secondly, there will be uncertainties and anxieties among members of the change unit about the nature of their task and the criteria for success, and consequently, tensions and conflicts may become manifest between members of the team. Next, unit members severally and collectively will suffer personal anxieties about their position in the company, the way they as individuals are being appraised in conditions of unusual vagueness and ambiguity, how they now fit, and will fit in future, into the status and power structure of the organization, and how appointment to the team has affected their chances of advancement. Finally, individuals are likely to experience internal stress and dissonance as their own value systems and perceptions of the wider organization and its behaviour patterns change and as they try to resolve some of the external causes of tension. As we explore the implications of the situation further, the sources of each of these strains become more evident, and the way that they interact with and feed back on each other can be understood.

THE PROBLEMS OF A CHANGE IN ROLE

Let us, then, begin to examine the characteristics of the management of change. The most striking is that it is a new role, outside the orthodox, more routine activities of the organization. When managers transfer to this new role, changes take place in their orientations; two processes can be identified. In the first place, the professional values and the disciplinary structure of thinking which they have held in their former positions give way, in the course of training and experience, to new concepts, new skills of analysis and of intervention, and new ways of thinking about organizational problems, which may well be at variance with their previous background and training. Secondly, as a result of stepping out from a routinized operation, such as production, marketing or personnel, into a more uncertain one where wider problems are being examined, using longer time scales, the member's perception of the organization as a whole, its structure, value system and authority pattern tends to change. The organization begins to be seen in a different context and from a different perspective than before. This second process is reinforced by the new learning which has taken place in the course of induction into the programme.

The change in values creates practical difficulties for members of the change team in that they tend to use a changed frame of reference, and even begin to speak a different language from other members of the organization. Difficulties arise in communication with former colleagues. However, in order to perform their task effectively they have to be in a position to influence others, to involve them and arouse their interest. In a sense, the task of remaining in contact with and able to influence other people in the organization becomes more difficult the more effective the unit is in socializing and giving new orientations to its own members. Here, then, is the source of three kinds of tension. The dynamics of value change and the increasing understanding of organizational complexities create psychological stresses within the individual; unit members discover that they have communication difficulties with those whom they need to influence; and anxieties among team members about effectiveness tend to occur as these communications difficulties become apparent.

THE OUTSIDERS WITHIN THE ORGANIZATION

If these were the only difficulties, they would probably be tolerated without too much trouble. They are the kind of problems met by many newly introduced disciplines: operations research or ergonomics practitioners may, for instance, meet many of them. However, when a rational attempt is being made to bring about change in structure, style or relationships, special difficulties arise. The external pressures which normally induce organizational changes to take place are absent, and all the pressures from within the existing social structure are to resist unnecessary modifications to relationships, to preserve what participants feel to be of most value to them, and to prevent characteristic modes of behaviour from departing too far from what is familiar and, therefore, relatively safe.(3) It is a most difficult form of intervention and, because the change agents themselves also need to preserve values, it may be impossible for planned change to be effected from within an established position. To be effective, it requires both willingness and ability on the part of change agents to divorce themselves from existing relationships and to stand outside a bureaucratic structure. There must be a perception, both on the part of members of the change programme and on that of their peers elsewhere in the organization, that they are in some way different from the rest.

This is in itself a source of stress. Complex industrial organizations are, by their nature, highly structured. Structure takes the form of well-defined lines of authority, well-defined areas of responsibility, control systems which regulate behaviour and define the criteria for evaluating performance. It helps to define status relationships and gives a fairly clear indication of the type of present-day behaviour which is likely to be approved. It also gives clues as to the qualities and behaviour patterns appropriate for promotion upwards through the organization and, of course, it provides the actual channels for promotion.

Much has been written about the adverse psychological effects of control systems and of authoritarian, hierarchical organizational structures in that, for instance, they promote dependent behaviour, give too little scope for initiative and creativity, and direct behaviour into paths which are too narrowly defined and often inappropriate for the task in hand: in Argyris' view,(4) they create conditions which could lead to psychological breakdown.

What is not generally emphasized is that structure can be a source of considerable security. Members of organizations rapidly become familiar with patterns of behaviour and formal relationships, quickly discover what is expected of them in the form of compliance with organizational norms, and usually adapt to the requirements of the existing structure. They come to accept the norms of the organizational culture, and this acceptance of the value system - and the support and the security it gives - are the greater the more consistent and integrated it is, and the longer its characteristics have remained recognizably the same.

It is in relatively stable, inflexible organizations, where the structure has offered most sense of security, that programmes of planned change probably have most potential. Change agents are likely therefore to think themselves particularly exposed and insecure in comparison to their colleagues who remain in the familiar hierarchy. Even though the unit may sit somewhat uneasily within, say, an established personnel function, it may not be accepted by that function as a legitimate or really useful part of it, and its members do not get the support expected from those fairly near to them. Individuals must therefore look for emotional support to their colleagues within the unit, in order to compensate for the lack of security coming from the organizational structure.

However, this need raises further difficulties. If members of the unit are exposed to all the sources of anxiety suggested in this chapter, they are less able to give emotional support to their colleagues, and may even tend to project some of their difficulties on to them. Moreover, even where managers in the unit, as they develop new skills and become clearer about their task, do see a need to establish close collegial relations between themselves, and begin to evolve freer, more supportive problem solving modes of behaviour, this change itself creates further dissonances. Firstly, new members joining the unit will find difficulty in adjusting to the new relationships, especially since they will retain a recognized status in the hierarchical system of the larger company. If a new member's formal status is fairly low relative to that of established members of the unit, few stresses may be caused, since the internal status of a new member is also likely to be fairly low. Indeed, the new member may be pleasantly surprised by the receptivity of his new colleagues and by his own ability to influence them. If, on the other hand, the new member's external status is fairly high relative to established members of the unit, he is likely to experience considerable shock because of the constant indications given to him by his colleagues of how they rate his knowledge, skill and usefulness within the team, and by the apparent assumption of greater understanding and skill on the part of people whom he would normally consider junior to him. Until this situation is accepted by all members of the unit, differences in external status may well cause stresses within the team.

Second, even when the internal stresses have been resolved, for both individual and team, the unit member is left with the problem of reconciling his role in the unit with the fact that his formal status and title still have some validity in the rest of the company. If these are low, he may find his expertise and potential contribution are not recognized by other elements in the hierarchy. If they are high, he may discover that he is given credit outside the unit for higher expertise and greater ability than he is credited with inside it, or than he actually possesses. It may be expected that he will 'take charge' of others in the unit and bring them to order. Further, he may be unable to play some of the roles taken by his colleagues, say in dialogue with subordinate levels. Authority relationships, it is felt, are not very helpful in getting other managers fully involved in ideas, or in convincing others of the need for sustaining change. This may be better achieved in peer group relations by discussion, argument and demonstration, rather than through the influence of status.

Moreover, it may fairly quickly become apparent to people in the rest of the company that some new forms of relationship exist within the change unit, and the rest of the company may not see these as legitimate.(5) Difficulties are then multiplied for those intent on making the role of the unit effective. Members of the unit may perceive themselves as losing credibility, and their ideas failing to gain acceptance, simply because they are perceived as being a 'strange group'. Anxieties within the team are likely to be increased.

The problems do not end there. Membership of the change programme does not preclude an individual from playing other roles in the organization - membership of committees, working parties, perhaps special investigation teams, connected with the more routine operations of the company. Individuals move back and forth between the unit and the more bureaucratic elements of the organization. What is acceptable and approved behaviour within the change programme, and when playing a role as a member of the change programme is probably unacceptable when the individual is playing one of these other organizational roles. There is a requirement on the individual to alternate between the behaviour required in his consultative role and the more conformist behaviour required in the bureaucratic role. This is a further source of internal stress. Again, since this alternation between roles is not necessarily perceived by outsiders, the role behaviour itself becomes ambiguous, and the person concerned may be seen to be unstable or unpredictable - conformist in one situation, arrogant or argumentative in another. His individual credibility and ability to influence may be reduced.

CAREER UNCERTAINTIES

There is another consequence of taking managers out of the structure to join a new unit. The people selected to be members of the change programme are likely to be young, successful managers from established positions, probably from a number of functions and disciplines, who are recognized by their superiors, and who perceive themselves, as having considerable potential for advancement. These managers are removed from positions where the criteria for success are relatively clear and where they have conformed to these criteria. They are transferred into a new role and a new situation where none of this applies, and where performance in previous roles appears irrelevant.

So, in addition to all the other uncertainties, career patterns for individuals are far less clear than before. Managers may well conclude that they can only get advancement within the company through an eventual transfer back into the function from which they were drawn - certainly a transfer back into the main bureaucracy. If this be so, a prolonged absence from that function may be a considerable disadvantage, and the individual is likely to establish close links with it, to behave in such a way as to maintain his reputation and acceptability with his former superiors. Another dilemma is thus posed for the individual, who in his present position may be expected to take risks - and occasionally to act as an irritant - in an attempt to change established relationships, and yet who sees for his future advancement in the organization the need to conform sufficiently to satisfy the expectations of former superiors. There may well be a desire to retain a foot in both camps, which necessarily reduces the effectiveness of the individual in his present role and may irritate his colleagues, as well as again creating dissonance for the individual himself.

RISK AND UNCERTAINTY IN THE TASK

I have implied that, to be effective in bringing about major changes, those engaged in the change programme must no longer necessarily conform with established expectations. One of their objectives would be to change those expectations: to begin to modify relationships throughout the hierarchy, and eventually to begin to influence the processes of decision making, and the behaviour patterns of various levels in the company. Not only, therefore, is the change agent somewhat apart from the hierarchical structure but he must quite explicitly have stepped out of the normal conforming patterns of behaviour and be seen as attempting to change those patterns.

Managers already in a situation causing anxiety, may see this nonconformist aspect of their new role as being fraught with risks, both to the individual and the group. Other factors increase these risks. Firstly, in the new situation, neither the change agents themselves, nor their superiors, will have established any clear expectations about what the task consists of, or, if each has established an expectation, these may well conflict; there will be no familiar framework provided by disciplines or professional norms already recognized in the company, within which they can work. The boundaries of the task will be quite vague and ill formulated, and it is likely that, whether they desire it or not, the change agents will soon perceive themselves, and be perceived by others, to be impinging on and interfering with the established responsibilities of other, more familiar areas in the organization. Secondly, the criteria for successful performance are unclear, and cannot be made clear, given the nature of the change programme.

Moreover, the stimulation of change is inherently one of the most uncertain of activities, and those involved will be continually aware of the dilemmas which face them. If they do not produce any obvious changes, they will not, by definition, have succeeded in their task. The credit for identifiable changes, if successful, will be (and probably should be) claimed by others, for only if those others accept the new processes as of their own creation are they likely to cooperate with, adopt and build on them. If, on the other hand, changes are stimulated which have led the organization into difficulties and uncertainties, the change programme itself is likely

to be identified as bearing the major responsibility
for these difficulties, and blamed for them. The
problem is that change and its attendant risks are
the principal objectives of managers involved in the
programme. With other functions and other roles,
the introduction of change and improvement takes its
place alongside other tasks. Competence is judged
on a wider variety of performance criteria, most of
them more easily measurable and certainly bearing
smaller risks. The feeling within the change unit
is that not only does the role entail stepping into
a high-risk area but that the risks have no compensation in any possibility of recognition through
success. This only serves to exacerbate the stresses
already existing in the programme.

THE PROBLEM OF LEGITIMACY AND ACCEPTABILITY

The question of credibility or of perceived legitimacy
creates one of the most difficult dilemmas for members
of the change unit. The changes in role which we have
outlined are probably recognized by members of the
new unit but, to those at superior levels, they are
more evident as changes in behaviour - and, probably,
unacceptable changes. In a traditional, bureaucratic
company a perception usually exists that knowledge
resides where decisions are made: often at the higher
levels of the hierarchy. If so, then it is hardly
legitimate to call into question either the decisions
which have been made or the considerations taken into
account in making those decisions. Much less is it
legitimate to call into question the value system or
the decision making processes themselves.

What in fact we are seeing is a conflict between
the perceptions held by the unit, of their objectives
and the methods needed to achieve them, and the perceptions held by higher levels in the organization.
Having been established with a broad remit to induce
change and improvement, the unit members begin to
acquire new knowledge, skills and understanding which
are likely to bring about a subtle change in their

definition of the objective, and a rather greater departure from the original conception of the methods they need to employ. What superior levels will expect from the unit, as from most of their advisers, will be advice on techniques, on structures and mechanisms, on the most efficient way of putting a certain decision into effect, or reaching a given goal. They do not expect their juniors to feel able to argue, discuss, attempt to put unfamiliar views to them and to change their perceptions, at least in realms such as decision criteria, styles of management, or the nature of controls. Necessarily, members of the change programme, recognizing that they have taken on this unfamiliar role, feel uncomfortable about it; and it is likely that the initial reaction of superiors to new forms of behaviour, particularly from individuals whom they already know, is hostile, so that the discomfort is magnified.

Given the assumption on the part of unit members that their objective is to change values and decision making processes, and given that these processes can only be changed if the activities and potential contributions of the unit are accepted as legitimate, unit members are faced with a real dilemma. If they put forward proposals or involve others in activities which lead to fundamental new thinking, their right to make such suggestions or engage in such activities - and even the basis of their methods and theories - are likely to be challenged, and their corporate identity, which has already come under attack, runs the risk of being destroyed altogether. If, on the other hand, they make only those recommendations or analyses which are perceived by their superiors to be legitimate, they may be accused of not making any progress towards their real objective. This dilemma is inherent in a programme of this kind. It overlays all the other causes of stress and anxiety for the members of the programme, and its resolution is a prerequisite to the resolution of many of the other causes of tension. The problem is greater as members become more committed to the programme's real objectives. It is one which recurs continually.

THE REDUCTION OF DISSONANCE

Enough has been said to illustrate some of the sources of stress likely to be experienced by managers in this kind of programme. Combined they amount to a formidable force. Now it is virtually impossible for a group of people to exist and maintain their cohesion for a prolonged period in a situation of considerable stress. Of necessity, members of the group are drawn to seek to reduce the tension that they are experiencing and, above all, to try to gain a certain measure of credibility and perceived utility in the rest of the organization. Acceptability is sought, partly to raise individual security and reduce anxiety, and partly to enable the unit, at least in the short-term, to work more effectively with others in the company. One way in which some of the personal stresses might be relieved is by frequent changes in membership of the unit. If the combination of tensions becomes intolerable for individuals after a period, then programmed movement back into line and staff functions will overcome this and have the advantage that these other functions are being 'seeded' with a sprinkling of people aware of and, presumably, sympathetic to the aims of the change programme. This has the disadvantage, however, of increasing the problems associated with induction; and though individuals may thus escape from barely tolerable stress, the stress on the unit itself, caused by the nature of its task and by structural factors, remains untouched. Moreover, it may create problems of continuity and consistency of approach, of retaining corporate learning.

So reduction of dissonance between the change unit and other parts of the organization may well be considered necessary if the work of the unit is ever to be accepted. The one factor which tells against attempts to reduce dissonance is the belief that the behaviour best calculated to reduce dissonance will lead to a reduction in the unit's independence and objectivity, and its ability to recognize needs and effect changes, and that this in turn will create new kinds of stresses once the movement away from the original objective is noted.

How this ever-present dilemma is resolved depends on the circumstances of particular change programmes. What may occur over a long period is the expenditure of a great deal of effort, in discussion, in experimentation and in individual consideration, to seek means to overcome this major problem and to search for alternative strategies which would create some leeway to allow the unit to build up credibility before again attempting to pursue the objective directly. The controversy may even encourage dissension within the change team and exacerbate personal anxieties and insecurity. There is a magnification of existing stress.

As a last resort, the unit may conclude - tacitly or openly - that the dilemmas can be resolved only if the change programme is able to achieve some displacement of its original goals. It may seek some new role to enable it to survive and to achieve a recognized place in the structure of the organization, without having to justify itself on the basis of success in achieving major cultural change. According to the degree of commitment of members of the change programme, a great deal of effort is likely to be put into devising a solution whereby, although the original goal may have to be abandoned or at least postponed for a very long time, the objective which is eventually achieved is one which is worthwhile and does not lead to a complete betrayal of the ideals of programme members. Indeed, this displacement of goals may be quite unconscious. The dividing line between a devious strategy to achieve success *via* the achievement of credibility, and the pursuit of credibility as an end in itself, is very unclear.

There are a variety of new roles open to a unit in this situation. Perhaps the most frequent choice is a contraction of unit activities into some field of human relations training or process consultancy activity, usually among the ranks of middle managers, who may be exposed to a series of training exercises in interpersonal competence, communications and consulting skills.(6) This choice has a number of advantages: it is likely to receive high-level support, since it conforms to the assumption that much organizational inefficiency is due to skill deficiencies on the part of middle management; it absolves the change unit from the exposure to which it is liable in actual involvement in organizational change; it is recognizable as a legitimate activity, since training already has an important place in organizations; and it may be possible to assume that, since today's junior managers are tomorrow's directors and senior executives, to train them in some of the skills and understanding which their seniors now lack will at least increase flexibility and efficiency in the future.

A somewhat similar alternative would be for the unit to transform itself into one charged with organizing and putting into effect an overall programme of management development (which is of course closely allied to organization development). Again, this is a fairly legitimate activity, and unit members may well believe the understanding they have developed of organizational needs to be extremely useful, if not essential, in devising a relevant programme of management education and training, and planning for future company needs.

Another possible choice for the unit is to try to gain the ear of key people in very senior positions in the company, and to organize themselves to play a useful role as staff advisers and assistants to board members on a variety of policy and planning matters in which their newly acquired expertise can manifest itself. The unit's influence is then indirect and exerted through advice, and members will make sure that the advice is limited to what is, for the moment, acceptable to the executive concerned. Nevertheless, it may be felt that gradually, over the course of time, this influence will be effective in changing perceptions at the highest levels in the organization and hence begin to transform the company from the top.

Yet another possibility for a change unit which has operated on and become expert in some of the principles of modern organization theory and organization design, could be to put itself forward to the company as a group of consultants in this area, and to lend its assistance to line and staff managers, to engineering designers or maintenance specialists in helping to solve problems of job structuring, reward systems design, supervisory and management structures and control systems, or other problems in organization design which frequently arise in large organizations. Again the rationale behind this choice would be one of gradual action: that by the unit's work in ongoing areas of the company, helping to effect improvements in the operation of those areas, overall performance will gradually be improved, those concerned in the area will see the activity, new though it is, as legitimate and imposing no threat to their own authority or competence, since the role is recognizably similar to that of industrial engineer or technical adviser. Appreciation of the expertise residing in the unit may spread by this means, without exposing it to the risks involved in responsibility for effecting change or managing the amended system.

CONCLUSIONS

This chapter has concentrated on the tensions and dissonances which can exist in a unit charged with the institution of organizational change, and I have suggested that those tensions have many sources and are of several kinds. The more carefully such a unit is designed for a task effectiveness and the more committed its members are to the objectives set for the unit, the more serious the stresses that it is liable to experience. If planned change is, then, to have a chance of success, a great deal of consideration has to be given to how the dissonances being created on the programme affect the ability of unit members to work towards their objectives. Possibly, also, the advantages of some alternative, less direct ways of inducing cultural change have to be considered: more partial and more gradual approaches, or approaches to planned change which include mechanisms designed to increase the receptivity of the organization to new ideas and new processes.

Certainly, one of the moves most likely to increase the chances of success would be for those near the top of the organization - in whose hands the original decision lies for instituting the programme - themselves to undertake a full and careful analysis of the needs and potential difficulties of such a programme, to look fully into the implications of the changes they desire, and to examine how they themselves can help to create conditions in which the programme may be expected to succeed. If, for example, senior executives were to develop, from the inception of the programme and as a result of their own study of the implications, changed styles and methods of decision making, and patterns of behaviour consistent with their own commitment to the need for change, at least some of the dilemmas facing members of the unit would be avoided or reduced. The example of the top, and the clear indication this would give of the behaviour patterns desired by the top, would support many of the efforts of those managing the change programme. This, however, would require a very high degree of insight and commitment on the part of senior people and, for a variety of reasons, it is rare for this to be achieved.

References

1 Among relatively few published case studies of planned change in the United Kingdom are E Jaques, *The Changing Culture of a Factory,* Tavistock, 1951; G N Jones, *Planned Organizational Change: A Study in Change Dynamics,* Routledge and Kegan Paul, 1968; A Flanders, *The Fawley Productivity*

Agreements: A Case Study of Management and Collective Bargaining, Faber, 1964; S Cotgrove, J Dunham and C Vamplew, *The Nylon Spinners: A Case Study in Productivity Bargaining and Job Enlargement*, George Allen and Unwin, 1971; P Hill *Towards a New Philosophy of Management, The Company Development Programme of Shell UK Ltd*, Gower Press, 1971.

2 The difficult position of the change agent has been reported most clearly with respect to the outside consultant, rather than the company manager. See, for example, E Jaques, ibid; C Sofer, *The Organization From Within: A Comparative Study of Social Institutions Based on a Sociotherapeutic Approach*, Tavistock, 1961; N G Davey, *The External Consultant's Role in Organizational Change*, Michigan State University Press, East Lansing, Michigan, 1971. Experience seems to show that the position of the internal manager of change is at least as delicate as that of the outside consultant, partly because he is less able to make apparent his differentiation from the rest of the organization.

3 A similar point is discussed in L E Greiner, 'Patterns of organizational change', in G W Dalton and P R Lawrence (with the collaboration of L E Greiner,) (eds), *Organizational Change and Development*, Irwin, Homewood, Ill., 1970, p 218ff.

4 C Argyris, *Understanding Organizational Behaviour*, Dorsey, Homewood, Ill., 1960.

5 A similar point is noted, in C Argyris, 'Today's problems with tomorrow's organizations', *Journal of Management Studies*, Vol 4, No 1, February 1967, 34ff.

6 See E H Schein, *Process Consultation: Its Role in Organization Development*, Addison-Wesley, Reading, Mass., 1969.

PART 3
ORGANIZATION
AND CULTURE

9

Structures, Process and Stress

Tom Lupton

The title of this chapter carries an invitation to assume that there is a connection between three abstract ideas, namely, structure, process and stress. More correctly, the assumption is that the events, activities and states of affairs to which the concepts refer are related, perhaps by chains of causation. In other words, the logical connection between the abstract ideas is a good reflection of the logic in events.

To examine this assumption seems worth while. If, on examination of the empirical referents of the concepts, we are able to suggest the existence of connections we may feel confident that our abstract reasoning reflects what goes on and, knowing this, we may embark on changes with assurance that we can anticipate some of the outcomes.

More concretely: suppose that we believe that *managerial stress* is an impediment to the happiness of managers and their performance in their jobs and, suppose also, that it can be shown that structure causes stress, then we may proceed to make structural alterations, in the knowledge that stress may be relieved and happiness and performance thereby improved.

Space is limited and the subject complex, so it seems sensible to proceed as follows. First, to define the three concepts in the expectation that some connection will be revealed. Second, to draw on some examples to illustrate the connections, or lack of them. Finally, to judge the implications for the practice of management and the training of managers.

DEFINITIONS

We can define *stress*, for our present discussion, as a set of forces acting on a person, the existence of which is identified by its effects. Leaving aside the nature of these forces, we know their effects by physical changes such as pallor, change of facial expression and bodily posture, withdrawal from social relationships, low task performance, impediments of speech, sighs, nervous laughter. These manifestations are usually described abstractly as anxiety, worry, emotional disturbance, aggression, withdrawal, tension, strain and so on, which are, in turn, sometimes thought to be the reason for certain physical malfunctions, stomach ulcers, for example, or heart conditions, or for obsessive behaviour such as heavy smoking and drinking.

The idea of *structure*, as it is generally conceived, refers to a set of parts linked according to some principle or principles to form a persisting whole.(1) When we speak of *social* structure, the parts referred to are social positions, not, we emphasize, individuals, but the positions they may occupy from time to time. The principles linking them may be, for example, kinship, or formal authority, or functional interdependence. In a manufacturing firm, positions such as machine-shop foreman, production planner, engineering manager, turner, and progress chaser, are linked by chains of formal authority and functional interdependence, *via* rules and procedures governing behaviour and the sanctions that are designed to influence behaviour. There are always other, less formally designed and imposed links forged by stable, mutual expectations and by custom and tradition. Like the formal, explicit rules, these customary norms impose constraints and present opportunities for the individual, which are external to him. In the family, positions of father, mother, brother, etc. are linked by formal (legal) rules, which set out mutual rights and obligations. There are, however, other equally compelling pressures on the individual arising from the social values he internalizes, to behave, for example, as a 'good son', or an 'exemplary parent'.

The existence of social structure is inferred from observations of what is said and done. It is an abstract idea, since it does not include all that could possibly be observed in social relationships, activities, or events. The signs of structure are, of course, behaviour that recurs, exhibiting pattern and regularity. The observer notes that the machine-shop foreman runs his shop according to schedules drawn up by the production planner, which may be issued every week (perhaps every day). This fact does not exhaust a description of the way that the machine-shop foreman runs his shop, nor does it include all the possible relationships of the foreman and the production planner. But it does express a persistent relationship of functional interdependence in which the production planner is formally defined as the initiator of action. This is so, whether in fact a specific foreman is less than meticulous in his adherence to the plan, or another chooses tacitly to ignore much of it, perhaps because of pressure from his subordinates to do so.

The engineering manager might be observed to call his plant engineers to a planning meeting each morning at ten. The observer notes that they usually turn up, listen and respond respectfully. He also notes that they send apologies if they are unable to come, and that some kinds of apologies are more acceptable than others. He concludes from this that the plant engineers 'report' to the engineering manager, that he is 'responsible' to the technical director for what they do and that he carries authority over them. This is a structured relationship, it has persistence, it recurs, it is a pattern of relationships governed by formally allocated authority and responsibility and it will continue in some form, even if a new man occupies the position, and retimes or even abandons the planning meeting. I must emphasize again that, because a relationship between positions is structured, this, theoretically, fully describes the relationship. But if it did in practice, then that organization would have succeeded in persuading human beings to act exactly as they are formally asked to behave, and to confine their behaviour entirely to that act. Obviously, in practice, this is rarely so.

When organizations are referred to as being 'highly structured', we mean that they have devoted a lot of attention to describing precisely the positions and the relationships between them in terms of tasks, rights, obligations, authority and so on, and have introduced administrative systems designed to ensure that the incumbents behave in ways that conform to the formal definition, and in no other way. Organizations that 'lack structure' are those in which the relationships observed to take place, although they may exhibit regularity, arise out of the perceptions and motives of individuals as to the tasks to be carried out, and the relationships of authority and technical independence that are necessary to carry them out. To anticipate a later point, managerial stress may occur in organizations with 'high structure' and 'low structure' alike, for different reasons.

The concept of structure, as defined here, is a static one. The observer abstracts a pattern from events and activities and describes it in timeless terms; 'this is the structure of British Rail', 'this is the structure of the Business School', for example. More commonly, in industrial and commercial organization, the 'structure' is exhibited as an organization chart (a static thing) and/or as a set of formal control systems, which are assumed not to be in process of change, whether they are or not.

The concept of *process* includes time.(2) The observer interested in process notes what is happening; he is highly sensitive to the way that events and activities are related to other events and activities in time sequence. There may be and usually are regularities, also cycles of events, cumulative processes such as self-fulfilling prophecies, virtuous and vicious circles, and so on. There may also be unexpected irregular conjunctions of activities and events, ie as they appear both to the observer and the participants, which lead to new turns of events.

Structure is an abstraction from process but, although both concepts are abstractions at different levels from a complex reality, they are present in the minds of the incumbents of positions and the participants in activities, relationships and events. An individual experiences the weight of authority and is influenced by events and his own and others' interpretations of them - in short by the social processes that involve him and from which he forms his values, beliefs and expectations.

STRUCTURE, PROCESS AND THE TRANSFER OF STRESS

By now, the reader will have perceived for himself some of the possible connections between structure, process and stress. Structure and process, and perceptions of them, could be a source of stress. Stress, and its consequences for individual behaviour and interpersonal and intergroup relationships, could be an influence on process, and process could be a creater and dissolver of structures. (see Figure 9.1).

For example, it is not difficult to see that the duties and obligations that partly define a social position, and the sanctions that go with breach of these, may be too much for any individual to cope with, or for any one particular incumbent. The failure of attempts to redefine the position, or to distribute the stress throughout the structure, may be a source of further stress. This, in turn, could lead to illicit manipulation of tasks and relationships in an organization, or to the displacement of the effects into other structures – the family, for example.

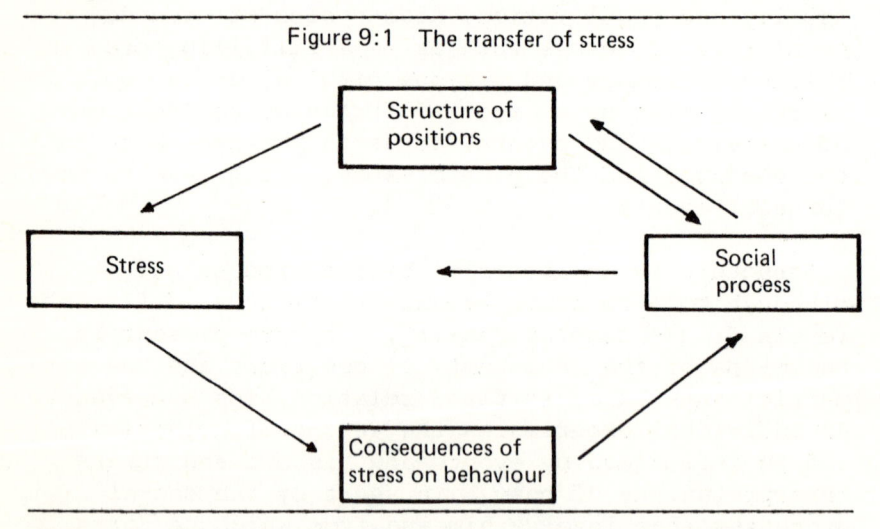

Figure 9:1   The transfer of stress

Systems of Management by Objectives, and other managerial control systems, can be used to illustrate some of these points. In MBO, where formal sanctions relating to promotion, pay and prestige may attach to formal assessment of performance, high structuring is entailed. Such systems are known to generate anxiety(3) and to encourage illicit manipulation of the system, much as blue-collar workers manipulate pay systems and procedures for allocating work, and managers bias estimates.(4) The exact effects of such manipulation on job satisfaction and task performance cannot be stated as universal propositions, since they depend on particular situations and persons, but it is possible to speculate that the result on both satisfaction and performance will not always be negative.

Of course, the processes of manipulation themselves exhibit regularities and have structure, and the effects of their persistence, however beneficial, may in some situations, transfer stress to the system initiators and designers and, in turn, lead to the generation of new systems which may or may not be efficacious. The motives for and sources of innovation, and the response to it, may be partly explained by reference to the idea of *stress transfer* through structure *via* process.

The connections that we have been exploring can be further illustrated by reference to a set of linked incidents (processes) which took place recently in a manufacturing plant:

1   Worker breaks factory rule

2   Foreman threatens worker with disciplinary action (to enforce conformity with factory code).

3   Worker refuses to conform. Foreman loses temper, using threatening language. Worker reports foreman to shop steward for breach of the rule which prohibits foreman from using threatening language.

4   Shop steward, according to formal procedure, raises matter with management, asking that foreman be disciplined. Higher management judges that foreman was not justified in using threatening language in the context of a minor infringement and, on the grounds that his actions seemed, in context of other recent events, to have alienated shopfloor opinion, transfers him temporarily from the workshop.

5   The foreman's union now demands that the foreman
    be reinstated, on the ground that the authority
    of all foremen will be undermined if he is not.

6   Top management now faces an acute dilemma. If it
    decides to reinstate the foreman to placate the
    foreman's union and to protect the foreman's
    authority as a member of management, then the
    workers' union will probably take action to pre-
    vent reinstatement, possibly by striking. If it
    decides not to reinstate, there is a danger that
    the foreman's union, which includes key
    technicians as well, will probably take militant
    action.

Note how the sequence of events is influenced by
structural factors. The foreman's exercise of
positional authority is challenged, he experiences
stress and exhibits some of its symptoms - aggression,
threats and so on. This is interpreted as a breach
of a formal rule and the behavioural norm. Under
further threat, the foreman seeks allies in his
union, so as to transfer the stress, by insisting on
the formal restoration of his positional authority.
The worker's union shifts it to the management, who,
after fruitless attempts to redistribute it in
accordance with the existing structure, suggest that
the problem be transferred out of the system to an
arbitrator. The arbitrator role is a stress absorber.
The arbitrator, because of his personal non-involve-
ment and the way that his position is structured by
his terms of reference, avoids undue stress himself.
He cannot, however, remove the causes of stress
unless he makes recommendations for structural change,
in which case he is assuming an innovative role.
Most arbitrators do, in fact, recommend changes.

   These events neatly illustrate the mutual inter-
connections of process, stress and structure. They
also introduce the idea of stress transfer as a
conflict-avoidance mechanism. Individuals must
relieve stress, either by adapting to it mentally
and physically, ie by internal changes of state,

hence the existence of so-called stress disorders, or by avoiding it through manipulations of personal relationships and structural configurations, *via* the initiation of new social processes. Individuals seek to satisfy moral dilemmas and their own personal needs to relieve anxiety and to resolve conflicting rational pressures to act, by using the power they possess, or can gain access to, to manipulate the social environment from which their difficulties are perceived to have come.

There are some cases, however, in which the avoidance of stress, or the relief of it, is only possible by complete personal withdrawal from the position, or by removing someone else from their position; in other cases, structural redistribution of the power to manipulate processes and structures is either demanded or offered as a solution. The following case illustrates both these processes.

The chief executive of a manufacturing company was formally responsible for the performance of that company to the chief executive of the large group to which the company belonged. Faced with difficulties in the product market and with pressures from the unions, which were exacerbated by complex work-flow and supply problems and low effort levels, and under insistent pressure for economic results from the Group, the chief executive tried several expendients of the 'high structure' variety, partly as a result of pressure from some of his own senior colleagues to 'bring the situation under control'. These did not seem to help much in relieving his personal dilemmas or his relationships with his colleagues, nor those with the unions, the work force and the Group chief executive. He eventually turned towards a solution which involved the distribution of power within the system and the introduction of flexible procedures for management and administration at the point of production by workers themselves, with a system of coordination from the 'bottom up'. To the extent that he was successful in alleviating his own anxieties by distributing stress (and the capacity to manage it) within the plant, he began to generate anxieties at group level about his own behaviour, which was perceived as a dangerous surrender of management control. Since he seemed unable to demonstrate satisfactorily that the undoubted improvement in relationships which occurred would be reflected also in economic results, he was subjected to criticism not only from his superiors, but from his own colleagues, whose reluctant support was now perceived by them as a danger to their own career prospects. In these circumstances, he was unable to carry through his undertakings to the work force and thought that he had no alternative but to resign.

Of course, that is not the end of the matter for the company, since whoever succeeds is faced not only with all the well-known problems of succession to high office,(5) but with the conflict arising from the sharply disappointed expectations engendered by the organizational experiment.

I shall not discuss this matter of participative management further, since it is dealt with in Chapter 6. My final section looks at some practical implications of the analysis.

CONCLUSIONS

If, during the analysis, I have conveyed any impression that the existence of stress in organizations is a moral blemish, I should correct it at once. Mild stress - or rather the desire to relieve it - is an energizing, not a debilitating force. Therefore, rather than organization design aiming to abolish stress, the intention should be to manage it effectively, so that the potential energy is effectively utilized without undue generation of more stress. The outcomes, furthermore, should be monitored for their effects on individuals - both as to stress signs and performance - and on organizational performance.

The generation of mild stress, if our analysis is sound, could be a matter of conscious design of structures, or perhaps it could deliberately leave them with some ambiguity while providing opportunities for informal discussion of the problems arising, and to follow up the resulting processes so as to discover what new structures are emerging, and with what consequences.

Beyond this, precise practical recommendations are not possible without close analysis of the situation to which they are to be applied. It cannot be otherwise, for reasons I have already given. This is why a good theory of structure, process and stress is a valuable tool for the practising manager, for without it, he cannot diagnose and prescribe beyond hunch and intuition.

References

1 For a discussion of the concept of *structure*, see R Boudon, *The Uses of Structuralism*, Heinemann Educational Books, 1971. (First published 1968 by Gallimard, *A Quoi La Notion De Structure*.) See also, H C Bredemeier and R M Stephenson, *The Analysis of Social Systems*, Holt, Rinehart and Winston, New York, 1962, pp 29-39.

2 For a discussion of the concept of *process*, and its relationship to *structure*, see W R Scott, *Social Processes and Social Structures*, Holt, Rinehart and Winston, New York, 1970, pp 141-5.

3 See, for example, J D Wickens, 'Management by objectives - an appraisal', *Journal of Management Studies*, Vol 5, No 3, October 1968, pp 365-79; also C F Molander, 'Management by objectives in perspective', *Journal of Management Studies*, Vol 9, No 1, February 1972, pp 74-81.

4 See, for example, A E Lowe and R W Shawe, 'An analysis of managerial biasing: evidence from a company's budgeting process', *Journal of Manage-*

ment Studies, Vol 5, No 3, October 1968, pp 304-15.

5   See, for example, A W Gouldner, *Patterns of Industrial Bureaucracy*, Free Press of Glencoe, New York, 1954. For some anthropological examples, see, M Fortes, 'Ritual and office in tribal society', in M Gluckman (ed), *Essays on the Ritual of Social Relations*, Manchester University Press, 1962, pp 53-88; also, J Goody (ed), *Succession to High Office*, Cambridge Papers in Social Anthropology, No 4, Cambridge University Press, 1966.

10

Stress and the Manager in the Over-Controlled Organization

David Weir

Widget Systems have got it all worked out. Their policy of relocating to a country site somewhere in the home counties, in the early fifties before it became a fashionable move, had enabled them to capture a work force consisting largely of young, skilled men who - like Widget - had moved away from the 'smoke' in search of something better. Twenty years later, many of these pioneers are still Widget men, stalwarts now and mildly contemptuous of their younger colleagues who do not recall the early days of innovation and expansion. But if Widget aren't the biggest payers locally they are among the steadiest, and labour turnover is satisfyingly low. For Widget are secure now; 'The Rolls Royce of the Widget Trade' is a slogan that even the personnel staff are pleased to intone in a slightly deprecating way so that you realize that deep down they do *honestly* think it is a damn good product. And it is... especially since the Widget Minor burst on the scene five years after the move and established Widget as an unrivalled leader in this small but utterly steady corner of the market. Sedulously avoiding diversification and takeover, Widget have remained what they always aimed to be, a highly successful medium-sized family firm. Control is firmly 'where it belongs', according to Widget's fifty-five year old chairman, *primus inter pares* of a small board of working directors. His philosophy is a simple one, 'Brains got us here, and planning keeps us here'.

Widget *is* planned too, and a bustling methods department backed by a small but high-powered operational research team provides the nerve fibres for management muscle. Their last major impact on the firm was about seven years ago when an outbreak of pilfering from the stores provided the opportunity for a re-examination of the systems for issuing parts and sub-assemblies to the line. The smaller components of the Minor *had* proved tiresome to manipulate but signing out replacements for 'damaged parts' had degenerated into a farce. A one-for-one system of exchange was instituted, with foreman and storekeeper sharing responsibility for signing. The loophole had been closed and the aberrant system brought under control.

But now Widget have problems again: the local police think the firm 'ought to know' that the Minor components are being openly sold in local pubs by employees. More disturbingly, a local 'cowboy' and fringe petty criminal had dropped into a discussion (of other matters of mutual concern to the force and himself) the fact that he knows someone who will 'knock off' anything from the firm, to order. The chairman's response is immediate and disbelieving, 'not us, not Widget; we know where every last nut and bolt is at any hour of the day or night.' But his confidence is not supported by the six-monthly figures which indicate a substantial stock deficit. Given the rising cost of materials, this is leading the firm straight for its first-ever serious loss.

'How did it happen? Why didn't anybody tell me?' the chairman murmurs as he surveys the wreckage. 'We didn't know either,' respond his colleagues, apparently hoping that the ritual incantation of collective ignorance will somehow atone for the chaos which has ensued. But all are agreed on what to do: tighten up; let them see that they cannot get away with it; restrict access to the stores to all but a chosen few whose trustworthiness can be assured; impose more effective controls on the movement of materials and parts.

ORGANIZATIONAL STRESS - A PROCESS OF DEFORMATION

What went wrong at Widget is not all that unusual and it may be symptomatic of something which, for want of a better term, we will call 'organizational stress'. But, before we go on to discuss it in more detail, let us distinguish between two different (and not necessarily related) ways in which we talk about stress. The expression is often applied to the effects of occupying a particular position in an organization. So we read of stress in the job of an airline pilot, or the stresses and strains of occupying a top managerial post. This is *individual* stress. Managers, of course, normally expect to occupy a position in which stress of this kind is one of the features. *Organizational* stress is a far more insidious phenomonon; it is the process by which a firm or institution becomes deformed, slowly and systematically, by the constant malfunctioning of some system. For a while, other systems take up the load and new, unofficial ways of adapting develop. Possibly the firm as a whole may benefit from the changes, especially if they are recognized as the results of inexorable and inevitable pressure, and the new ways are adapted into the firm's procedures; the vices are transformed into virtues. But often, the firm fights against the deformities. Conceivably, it gets involved in radical and major surgery. More often, it reacts by a reaffirmation that the old medicine really will work - given time and a stricter adherence to the prescribed dose - and fails to recognize stress as symptomatic of a need to adapt to changing circumstances.

The problem for Widget can be stated simply. Despite the apparent clarity and rigour of the system for controlling the issue of stock and parts, it was not functioning effectively. Management in fact was in ignorance of the *real* stock position at a particular point in time. The problem is not merely that the employees were redistributing the stock in their favour, but that management did not know that this was happening. Moreover, to respond by tightening up invited the possibility that even more subtle and ingenious stratagems for circumventing the operation of the system would be developed by the employees.

It is not our purpose here to go into the techniques of malfeasance in the stores or to speculate about the ways in which random pilfering escalates into carefully organized systematic theft.* What we are concerned with at this point is to explain some of the consequences of this type of behaviour for the organization, and why we feel justified in describing this problem as one of 'organizational stress'.

DEVIATIONS FROM THE RULES

The trouble is that Widget's system is, in a sense, *overcontrolled*. It is simply too laborious and time consuming to go through the appropriate and proper channels. In the interests of maintaining production, foremen and employees have connived at the development of a multiplicity of ways of circumventing

---

*Within the scope of a short chapter it is impossible to do more than sketch out embryonically a way of approaching a problem, but in a forthcoming publication these topics will be explored in more detail.

168

official routine. But the fact that management
apparently sets such store by correct procedures
poses something of a problem: to get round it, foremen and storekeepers connive to produce statistics
which are at best irrelevant, at worst a carefully
manipulated prediction of the figures that management
was expecting anyway. Management is inclined to
attach credence to these statistical fictions without
inquiring further into their origin.

   Actually, in terms of production, it may be simpler
and more efficient for employees *not* to follow the
rules. So, for instance, foremen and workers learn
that they have to build up a buffer stock of parts
and spares in order to maintain continuity of production. Further, the one-for-one exchange system
may be perverted into a ritual presentation of a
'time-honoured' **part** which has gone the rounds
several times before.

   Storekeepers have their own ways of meeting this
attack on their collective virtue. Many organizations
subscribe to the doubtless mythical story of the
archetypal storeman who kept as essential equipment
a sheet of tracing paper on which to record the
outline of returned parts for which an exchange was
claimed. Other storemen react by simply being
obstructive, reasoning that if the problem really is
as urgent and immediate as is claimed, they will be
bound to be furnished with the 'further and better
particulars' that their legalism requires. Still
others resort to the blind eye, apparently sub-
scribing to the theory that parts which are stolen,
mislaid or otherwise 'wasted' or 'shrunk' somehow
constitute less of a problem than those which are
issued in good faith under conditions which do not
quite match up to the most rigorous interpretation of
the rule book.

   Although we are using inadequacies in a system of
stock control as an example of the fund of stress
which results from what we have labelled an over
controlled situation, there are several other
symptoms of this insidious and damaging problem, and

many other ways that it can surface - for example, in
overt crime. In a study of an aircraft manufacturing
plant in the US, Bensman and Gerver(1) show how a
rigorous and systematic system of inspection of
finished components could quite readily be circum-
vented by the production operatives with the covert
connivance of the foreman. The result was that a
serious and potentially lethal organized 'crime' -
'tapping' a stop nut in order to insert a bolt into
a section that had been incorrectly aligned - was
rampant throughout the plant. As the authors point
out:

> The use of the tap is the most serious crime of
> workmanship conceivable in the plant. A worker
> can be summarily fired for merely possessing a
> tap. Nonetheless, at least one half of the work
> force in a position to use a tap owns at least
> one. Every well-equipped senior mechanic owns
> four or five of different sizes and every
> mechanic has access to and, if need be, uses them.

This apparently bizarre juxtaposition of honesty and
deviance is in practice very common indeed, as we are
all aware. What is perhaps surprising is that we often
fail to recognize it for what it is, an indication of
a distortion in the operation of a system as a whole,
rather than some aberrant excrescence which has
inflicted itself on us. As Bensman and Gerver put it,

> ...deviant actions are not a separate category of
> actions, defiant of the central ends of a total
> system, but are simply part of the totality of
> actions that make up the hundreds of individual
> transactions in an organization.

Actually, the kind of perversion of the system we are
describing here is rather akin to what has become
known as 'secondary deviation', following the work
of Lemert.(2) He argues on a wider theme that
'society's efforts to alleviate social problems of
deviants through the establishment of public policy
may aggravate or perpetuate the problems.' When

situations of this sort develop, they tend to share certain common features.

LEARNING TO BEAT THE SYSTEM

The newcomer to the factory is shown and taught how to use the correct procedure. But he soon learns that to follow procedures causes him a certain amount of aggravation with his colleagues and foreman. If he takes the initiative himself, he may be regarded with some suspicion by the storekeeper. The latter's philosophy inclines him to the view that his stores are under constant threat of attack from the subversions of dangerous men who dream, night and day, of new devices for extracting stock without going through the proper procedures. And the newcomer learns, too, that the appropriate view to hold of the storekeeper is that he is a reactionary and unconstructive character to whom a good store is one in which items are kept - and from which they are never issued. The newcomer learns that a bigger stock of his own is one way of circumventing these embarrassing and time-consuming confrontations with the guardians of the stores. So he starts to conform to the storekeeper's expectation of him and takes his first steps towards learning how to beat the system.

Of course, if everybody is beating the system in this way, then it makes little sense to talk of a 'system' at all. But it is really too much trouble and not worth the while of anybody in particular to blow the whistle until the thing gets really out of hand, by which time the people who know most about it have most to lose by drawing attention to the existence of some practice in which they are heavily implicated. An incidental result is that a philosophy of disdain approximating to contempt grows up around the activities of systems analysts, consultants, and methods teams in so far as the activities of these groups are directed towards the systems which should operate - or apparently exist on paper - and those which everybody knows to be operative.

THE SEARCH FOR A SCAPEGOAT

When the problem gets too big to be ignored, the search for a scapegoat is on. The platitudes fall like confetti: 'isolated instance', 'one bad apple', and one senses that, to some managers, the ideal culprit would be an evilly disposed long-haired teenage recruit, taking time off from football hooliganism to 'put the boot in' on an unsuspecting firm. Another scenario would see the threat in an aged incompetent soured by management's justifiable refusal to award an ill-deserved promotion. Possibly the explanation is thought to lie in someone who didn't know the ropes - the prescribed solution in this case is training and education. At all events, someone can usually be found who satisfies the classical recipe for the scapegoat - an outsider, a deviant and one whose services can most readily be dispensed with. Usually, however, the master deviants turn out to be none of these, but to be drawn from the same pool as that which produces the good, able workman, the long-serving employees; in short, those who have the knowledge, experience and trust to operate the system effectively. While it is tempting to try and separate the deviant system *analytically* from the ideal practice of how the organization as a whole operates, observation of how the thing works on the ground may lead to the conclusion that the persons involved in both are one and the same.

SUFFICIENT UNTO THE LEVEL IS THE PROBLEM THEREOF

The consequences of taking a problem to the next higher level of management may be rather negative for the individual concerned. He tries to find a way round minor and random fluctuations of materials and parts. He does not wish to become known as a man who is flummoxed or put out of sorts by the lack of a

Widget. Nor does he wish to establish a reputation for running to his foreman because the system is holding him up. (Conversely, his foreman's reputation depends on his *knowing* how things are, without having to be officially informed.) Neither does he want to become stereotyped as one of these cranky autocratic Victorian taskmasters who would not let his men take any decision of any moment in relation to their own job. And at the top, the works manager's concern with production and output may persuade him to turn a blind eye to the vague suspicion he has that all is not going according to the book. He may console himself with the reflection that the odd Widget here and there keeps the lads happy and, if it ever got out of hand, he would be the first to hear of it.

THE PRINCIPLE OF MINIMUM KNOWLEDGE

The organization sets great store by its control system, and even awards severe punishment for those infractions of its rules which come to light. However, typically, problems are usually solved by some kind of short-circuiting procedure at lower levels. These short circuits often involve breaking one of the rules. So there is no inducement for the man who really does know how Widgets are got out of the stores to share this information with his superiors. There will always be a sort of 'information bubble' trapped down between the lower layers of the system.

THE BELIEF IN THE SUPERIORITY OF SYSTEMATIC IGNORANCE

Management is quite often far from disconcerted that it has no knowledge of what ordinary workers take for granted. Indeed, managers may come to treat such lack of knowledge as a positive virtue, liberating them from too-blinkered a reliance on everyday operations and releasing them to concentrate their effort on policy, strategy and long-range planning.(3) The kind of knowledge which lower participants in the system do have tends to be dismissed as unimportant as,

indeed, may well be true in terms of specific cases.
But this disregard can lead to a systematic neglect
of the most important source of information - people.
Sadly, management education and even the business
schools do much to foster this regrettable tendency
to prefer the five-pound word of the dubiously academic
to the two-pence word of the rudely mechanical. Thus
managers may become irascibly contemptuous of the
admitted inadequacies of the kind of partial knowledge which can be derived from vehicles such as the
attitude survey, and opt in preference for the
intellectual rigour of almost total ignorance. Armed
with the shield of quantification and the sword of the
mathematical model they go forth to do battle with
demons, while small industrious mice nibble unnoticed
around their defences.

MISINFORMATION. STRATEGIES

As random, unsystematic subversions of the rules tend
to go unnoticed, the lower participants' activities
build up into a repertoire of devices for getting
round the regular procedures. Many of these are
perfectly legal, often improvements on management's
grand design, but others involve collusion and joint
action to do something not quite covered by the
official plan. Because management did not think to
institute measures to provide accurate information,
nobody knows the real answers to the 'how many?',
'how often?', or 'who?' kind of questions. But
management *does* require information on other things
in order to be assured that it is in control of the
situation. So pseudo-data on pseudo-events are
recorded, collated and, finally, with due seriousness
and solemnity, passed to higher levels of management.
But, in practice, even such an apparently innocuous
and 'objective' measure as a scrap rate or wastage
index is a constructed thing, produced according to
certain recipes as a result of the interaction of
several individuals who are sedulously engaged in...
producing a given rate of wastage. The fact that,
when the rate finally appears in all its statistical

glory, it approximates to the level predicted may be
not so much a tribute to the omniscience of management as a reminder of the power of estimation and
nice judgement of the operatives working in the area
concerned.

MINIMAL MONITORING BASED ON MISINFORMATION

Clearly, if its decision making capacity is a function
of the level of information, management is eventually
going to be severely handicapped by being at the
wrong end of a misinformation chain. It becomes
progressively more difficult for the organization to
monitor its own processes because the real decisions
are never adequately identified. In practice, top
management may become more constrained and defensive
in its decision making, while real discretion is
significantly more apparent at the lower levels. In
the example of Widget Systems, the ordinary workers
are confounding Maslow, Herzberg, North Paul and
others, by increasing their economic return in a way
that also allows for a fair amount of individual
entrepreneurship, as well as a substantial job
enlargement.

STRESS AND THE MANAGER

Stress, according to the medical dictionary, is a
condition characterized by tension and anxiety and is
not uncommonly associated with depression. The
manager in the kind of organization that we are
discussing is, of course , endemically liable to meet
these problems in his decision making role.(4) But
some especially provoking situations which are
particularly likely in the overcontrolled organization are liable to expose him to stress.

The Discovery Syndrome

It sometimes occurs that a manager happens on an
understanding of how things really work by uncovering

a practice which contravenes some rule of particular significance in his own personal philosophy. It may be for example, a breach of a safety regulation. No amount of assurance that 'It's always been done like this' or 'No ones lost a hand yet' can entirely banish the spectacle of himself in the crowded courtroom, facing the judge's angry cry, 'You mean to tell the court that you, a man of considerable education and occupying a position of responsibility for which you were doubtless handsomely remunerated, knew of this practice and allowed it to continue.' Yet the manager is aware that, so far, nobody *had* lost a hand and that you cannot stop a whole line just to ensure that all the safety guards are fastened down. The result is, not infrequently, stress. He decides to do nothing, but inevitably, tension and anxiety are created.

Failure of the 'New Broom'

A different form of stress ensues from the manager's attempt to project himself into the front line and take charge of the situation. Here he faces a characteristic dilemma of an intrinsically stress-provoking kind. If rapid action to excise the cancer is taken on first discovery, the manager risks the accusation that he is trigger happy and hasn't studied the problem sufficiently. And this may be true, for there is a danger that his initiative may meet an equally swift response resulting in the disappearance of the symptom rather than the underlying need for the practice. The tendency then will be to do something which is just adequate while hoping that the effects do not cause a widespread backlash. Either way, the manager is likely to create antagonism.

The Shot in the Dark

In practice, either of the above extreme reactions is less likely to occur than a third. The manager becomes aware gradually that he is somehow out of touch, that his attempts to innovate are frustrated not by surly negativism or rational dissent, but by a cheerful bland acceptance that he learns to recognize as signalling, 'Of course we will do as you say, provided that you accept that we are going to carry on as we are doing'. He either retreats into a pose of baffled resignation, accepts the *status quo* and becomes an avoidist* or embarks on the perilous course of intervention, feeling like one of those chaps who has to grapple with radioactive material, using tongs at the end of gloves into which at two or three removes the hands are inserted. Likewise, his sense of organizational touch is cripplingly attenuated.

CONTROL OVERKILL AND ORGANIZATIONAL STRESS

Practices such as pilfering, 'old soldiering' and the creation of buffer stocks, occur in many organizations and across a wide range of industries in both the private and public sector.(5) Typically, however, we would expect to find them in the kind of situation I have described as overcontrolled. One of the results of the kind of control overkill, which firms like Widget Systems develop, is that management becomes systematically unaware of how the organization is actually operating, and thus loses the capacity to make significant interventions to correct distortions which occur. In time, these distortions become incorporated into the operating procedures of the organization. Where these procedures differ to a measurable degree from the course which management is attempting to steer, a situation of organizational stress exists. The consequences for the manager whose responsibility it is to deal with this problem are likewise stressful.**

---

*A term I owe to discussions with W A Speck of the University of Newcastle.

**I am grateful for comments and suggestions made by Dan Gowler and Karen Legge in the preparation of this chapter. I am also glad to have had the benefit of helpful discussions with Tony Eccles. I owe the discovery of Widget, an anonymous and pseudonymous firm to my colleague, Tom Lupton, who first drew attention to its organizational eccentricities. Any reference to real life is purely intentional. The names have been changed to protect the guilty.

Refernces

1   J Bensman and I Gerver, 'Crime and punishment in the factory: The function of deviancy in maintaining the social system', *American Sociological Review*, Vol 28, No 4, December 1963, pp 588-98. (Reprinted in P Worsley (ed), *Problems of Modern Society*, Pengiun, 1972, pp 357-367.) On deviancy in industry, see also, S Dinitz, R R Dynes, A C Clarke, *Deviance: Studies in the Process of Stigmatization and Societal Reaction*, Oxford University Press, 1969; M Dalton, *Men Who Manage: Fusions of Feeling and Theory in Administration*, Wiley, New York, 1959; H Beynon, *Working For Ford*, Pengiun, 1973.

2   E M Lemert, 'The concept of secondary deviation', in E M Lemert, *Human Deviance, Social Problems and Social Control*, Prentice-Hall, Englewood Cliffs, N J, 1967, pp 49-52. (Reprinted in E Butterworth and D Weir (eds), *Social Problems of Modern Britain*, Fontana, 1972, pp 429-33.)

3   See, for example, W H Reid, 'Upward communication in industrial hierarchies', *Human Relations*, Vol 15, No 1, February 1962, pp 1-15.

4   See, for example, L R Sayles, *Managerial Behavior: Administration in Complex Organizations*, McGraw-Hill, New York, 1964.

5   See, for example, G Turner, *The Car Makers*, Eyre and Spottiswoode, 1963.

11

Expectations, Chance and Identity-Stress

Eileen Fairhurst

For some managers, it is a matter of conventional wisdom that stress is an occupational hazard, part and parcel of their job. Unfortunately, stress is a notion which has acquired a status out of all proportion to its usefulness. Its adoption into common and regular parlance has attributed it with panacea-like qualities. One of the most perplexing yet tantalizing features of its usage is its meaning. What does the concept of stress involve?

The orientation I wish to emphasize in this chapter is that stress is inextricably tied to the notion of self-identity. Now the formulation of the self, the personality, does not rest on some kind of cataclysmic event which, once conceived, remains untouched until the end of time. Our beliefs and behaviours do change over time, and attempts to explain these changes in terms of inadequate internalization or socialization, or by some residual notion of values, are not acceptable. In many ways, we behave in a chameleon-like manner, with our actions contingent upon the situation in which we are - and particularly the way in which we define that situation.

For example, the explanation that X failed in his job because he was stubborn so that he was unable to change his course of action simply begs the question. If X's position in the company was at the interface between various departments, he may have been faced with formidable role conflict. In satisfying the demands and expectations of one department, he may have been sowing the seeds of his own destruction: for one set of actions are deemed acceptable by one department yet unacceptable by another. These unacceptable actions are said to emanate from his stubborn personality and may lead to such statements as, 'After all we did warn him what would happen if he wasn't flexible.' Clearly, production managers may find themselves in such a situation. Similarly, foremen can be presented with considerable role conflict. They have the often conflicting expectations of both managers and workers to fulfil.

The point I am leading up to is that, rather than picturing identity as a totally idiosyncratic and enduring phenomenon, we should also consider structural influences on the development of self-identity, the personality. Becker and Strauss(1) offer an interesting perspective on this area of self-identity and its development. They suggest that the structural concept of career with its implication of movement from one status to another, associated with certain temporal features, provides a useful starting point for the study of personal identity. Occupational careers involve change from one job to another, usually within some kind of time perspective. Such a change affords experience to be gained, which then becomes the basis for a further move. Becker and Strauss see these features as also characteristic of change and development in self-identity. In this chapter, however, I am concerned not so much with the development of identity *per se*, the plotting of its course, but rather with the conditions under which stress may occur '...when an individual has to take stock, to re-evaluate, revise, resee and rejudge'.(2)

We all have many identities, eg wife, mother, friend, but, for our purposes, I intend to confine my remarks to the problem of identity-stress among managers. Work is one of the main spheres of activity from which man in industrial society gains his identity: to a large extent, man is - as perceived by himself and others - what his work is.

Sociological analysis of identity-stress has been mainly restricted to that arising out of professional socialization.(3) Both Coser(4) and Davis(5) have identified evasiveness as a response to identity stress. Olesen and Whittaker(6) provide a delightful example of student nurses' reaction to stress in terms of laughter: to burst into laughter is seen as a way of extricating oneself from uncomfortable situations.

In pre-industrial societies, perceived stressful relationships are institutionalized in the form of joking relationships; stressful situations are faced full on. In our society, perhaps the only such institutionalized relationship is that between married couples and parents-in-law: mother-in-law jokes are an integral part of many a comedian's act.

The high incidence of coronary thrombosis among managers is said to be caused by the increasingly stressful work of such men. Of course, the most effective way of dealing with stressful situations is to avoid them completely. In this chapter, I want to consider one further response to identity-stress, that of luck-labelling. By this I mean that incidents or experiences are accounted for in terms of work*

*I first became interested in luck as an accounting mechanism when analysing the career choices of doctors in some research I have done on medical careers.(7).

CONDITIONS UNDER WHICH STRESSFUL EXPERIENCES MAY OCCUR

Stress arises when there is no isomorphism between actions and the expectations of those evaluating actions. In the work situation, this evaluation will be done by both the actor (in one case, the manager) and by his superior. Now evaluation is a processual concept: it takes place over time. An integral, though not necessary feature of this time period may be an element of change.

The criteria for evaluation may be different from one time period to another. The structure from which expectations are generated may be changing. If this is so, the actor has to make some sense of the situation with which he is confronted. He has to reconcile the fragmentation of what is happening with the process that is causing the upheaval.

It is obvious that all instances of disjunction between self-perception of expectations and their perception by others will not always lead to stressful situations. Some have more efficient coping mechanisms than others: these are not uniformly distributed throughout the population. I would like to suggest that the following organizational circumstances may be related to managerial perceptions of identity-stress: the nature of the task, the promotion system characteristic of an organization, and conditions of uncertainty both within and outside the organization.

Promotion System

It is only fairly recently that management development programmes have been introduced into UK organizations. Such procedures are bureaucratic in form, so that they provide - or claim to provide - objective criteria by which a manager can be deemed ready for promotion. One ramification of relatively clear-cut criteria is that not only do they enlighten the successful but also those who fail. The unsuccessful are able to use these criteria in their own evaluation of what happened, and a potentially stressful situation may be avoided.

Promotion systems based on more competitive criteria may, however, have the adverse effect. Where criteria are unwritten and more amorphous, there is far greater scope for the unsuccessful candidate's self-evaluation to be couched in terms of personal failure. So, whereas this situation may prompt an unsuccessful candidate to indulge in soul-searching of the 'where did I go wrong'kind, the former situation would more likely lead to a statement such as, 'I now know that I must do something about a, b, c and d before I'm likely to get promotion'. Management development programmes are mechanisms through which potentially stressful situations can be minimized. On the other hand, more open promotion systems are, by their very nature, inherently stressful.

Conditions of Uncertainty

The notions of uncertainty and risk are very much a part of any analysis of organizations. Their usage, however, is surrounded by fuzziness. The distinction made by the classical economist, Knight, is particularly useful, for he clarifies and separates the differences between these two concepts. To him, decision making is characterized as risk taking when

> ...the distribution of the outcome of a group of instances is known while in the case of uncertainty this is not true, the reason being in general that it is impossible to form a group of instances, because the situation dealt with is in a high degree unique.(8)

Knight's conceptualization is sharply contrasted with everyday usages of risk, referring to 'any sort of uncertainty viewed from the standpoint of the unfavourable contingency' and 'uncertainty as to the favourable outcome'.

Clearly, most organizations operate with both risk and uncertainty. Many aspects of corporate planning are based on risk taking, for future policies and planning are founded on past performance: the outcome of certain actions are known.

On the other hand, it is in situations, for example, of innovation that uncertainty comes into play. In innovative periods, the changes involved are not only those of switching resources from one activity to another. Implementation of change impinges on more than the organization; it may present a manager with a stressful situation. In some organizations, a manager may be associated with a particular technique. So convinced is he of the usefulness of that technique that he literally stakes his career and, consequently, his identity on it. If the time comes, though, when it is decided that some aspect of production, contingent upon that technique, should be changed, one result would be a questioning by the manager of his identity. The foundation from which his work identity has grown (from which his identity has been nurtured and flourished) is threatened.

Nature of the Task

In many ways, stress arising from the nature of a task is similar to that discussed above. But here, stress arises from the task itself rather than from conditions of uncertainty associated with the task.

We might expect that in organizations where the quality of the finished product is contingent upon the quality of raw materials used in manufacture, stressful conditions may occur. In the latter example, the task is characterized by risk since the statistical outcome of the process is known. It is the extent to which unforeseen complications arise that is linked with potential for stress. For example, fluctuating quality in raw materials has far-reaching implications for continuous-process industries.

LUCK-LABELLING AND IDENTITY-STRESS

So far, I have briefly sketched out potentially stressful situations for managers. We can now focus our attention on luck-labelling as a response to identity stress. When somebody is in a stressful situation, a paramount concern is preservation of identity. Self-doubting and 'who am I?' questioning may mark such experiences.

For instance, in our society, adolescence is seen as an acutely stressful period. Not expected to act as a child but not yet accorded the status of an adult, the adolescent is faced with the problem of self-identity. Adolescence is a time when the adolescent asks of himself and others, 'Who am I?' We accept that adolescent behaviour may display contradictory features. Action which may be intended as appropriate to an adult may rather be deemed as inappropriate and that expected of a child. Indeed, adolescent attempts at preserving an identity, while at the same time seeking and groping for another, are institutionalized in phrases providing a rationale for action. Thus, phrases such as 'he's only going through a phase' not only acknowledge that some change is in process but also underline that such a period has some kind of time dimension attached to it.

I want to suggest that one of the ways that managers may attempt to preserve their identity is to account for events in terms of luck. An examination of some uses of luck will, I hope, make this clear.

When luck is used as an accounting mechanism — 'I was just unlucky I lost my job' or 'didn't get that job' — it may imply that the event occurred outside of, apart from, one's self. In other words, the responsibility for that event was not one's own. Now, we live in a culture where 'why' questions are expected to elicit a 'because' answer; it is assumed that actions are prompted by reasons. Pinpointing an event as due to luck then not only means that an explanation/account can be given but that the self can be maintained. The very fact of giving an answer admits that some part of the self is still firmly located in the society from which the self is generated.

In this way, some kind of baseline or springboard for the development and continuity of identity is provided. The actor is allowed a breathing space for a re-evaluation and re-presentation of self. Attributing something to luck may 'take the heat off' the manager. It has already been emphasized that we have many identities. A claim such as, 'I've lost my job but I'm lucky; I still have my health and family' acknowledges this. One identity, that of the breadwinner, is substituted for another - the healthy man and family man. More important, it is only the individual, the self, who can indulge in this situation. The individual stands outside himself by examining that specific sphere of activity or experience which has lead to the questioning of 'the self'. He plays one identity against another, and luck is the mechanism which he uses.

When a manager is faced with identity stress, the concept of commitment may be of great value to him. Like the idea of stress, this notion of commitment presents us with endless problems of meaning. Here, I am following Becker's ideas, so that commitment involves following a consistent line of activity in association with the same goal in varying situations.(9) Commitment to some goal may enable the manager to 'weather the storm' in a stressful situation as he perceives himself to be pursuing the intended course towards goal attainment. 'I've had an unlucky break but that won't stop me'. Reference to luck may be one manifestation of the manager's commitment.

Just as in adolescence, there is some kind of time constraint associated with societal tolerance of 'inappropriate' adolescent behaviour, so, too, is there a time dimension associated with acceptance of luck-labelling. We are prepared to accept that people have runs of good or bad luck - that something happened 'because I was lucky' or 'unlucky', as the case may be. But, after so long, we start to question the ability of the person constantly relying on luck as an accounting mechanism. This is particularly noticeable in sporting activities. After, say, six defeats on the run, we are no longer willing to accept that our favourite football team are having a run of bad luck but begin to question the ability of both players and managers. We have the paradox, therefore, where luck-labelling may not only maintain or provide the bridge for the emergence of a new identity but also incorporates a time dimension into its appropriateness as an accounting mechanism for the occurrence of events.

Identity-Stress and Mental Instability

I have emphasized that we all have many identities to call on in times of stress. It is only when a number of these identities do not provide a back-up or bridge for the development of new identities that we should even begin to consider linking mental instability with an inability to cope with stressful situations. Here a note of caution is necessary. To travel the explanatory path of mental instability is to embark on a journey fraught with immense difficulties. Nor is this the place to go into an elaborate discussion of the point. Suffice it to say that there is an extensive body of sociological literature which documents the complexity of illness definition and, especially, illness as legitimating failure.(10) Exhortation to dismiss mismanagement or bad management as resulting from a low tolerance of stress, derived from mental instability, should be treated with the contempt that it deserves.

Plausibility of Luck-Labelling and Identity-Stress

A predominant and major theme running through this chapter has been the multifaceted identities of social man. Furthermore, the work he does is a prime source of man's identity in Western industrialized society: the work ethic is a strong value. Now, if a manager is experiencing difficulties, however defined, in his identity arising from his work, he faces a dilemma. How can he account for his experiences without retaining some attachment to those experiences of the work world from which his identity has been partly formed? He knows all too clearly that his future identity is partially contingent upon any subsequent employment he will undertake. It is plausible that accounts of his present predicament could be framed in terms of luck for,

> As in many other areas of social life the labelling process functions to tidy up the bookkeeping of a society riddled with value inconsistencies. That those excluded from participation would seek these labels is a natural outcome of the process.(11)

The point about luck is that it does offer an acceptable rationale for certain predicaments. And particularly so in a society like ours which requires identification of motives for action; 'why' questions carry an implicit demand for a 'because' answer.(12)

References

1   H S Becker and A Strauss, 'Careers, personality and adult socialization', in H S Becker (ed), *Sociological Work*, Allen Lane, 1971, pp 245-60.

2   A Strauss, 'Transformations of identity' in A Rose (ed), *Human Behaviour and Social Processes*, Routledge and Kegan Paul, 1972, p 71.

3   For another perspective on the development of self which focuses on the idea of career, see Goffman's discussion on the moral career of inmates in total institutions, in E Goffman, *Asylums: Essays on The Social Situation of Mental Patients and Other Inmates*, Pelican, 1971.

4   R Coser, 'Evasiveness as a response to structural ambivalence', *Social Science and Medicine*, Vol 1, 1967, pp 203-18.

5   F Davis, 'Uncertainty in medical prognosis, clinical and functional', in E Freidson and J Lorber (eds), *Medical Men and their Work*, Aldine-Atherton, Chicago, 1972, pp 239-48.

6   V Olesen and E Whittaker, 'Adjudication of student awareness in professional socialization: the language of laughter and silence', *Sociological Quarterly*, Vol 7, No 3, Summer 1966, pp 381-96.

7   For an explanation of the luck phenomenon, see Eileen Fairhurst, 'Luck, choice and medical careers', unpublished paper, Manchester Business School, 1974.

8   F Knight, *Risk, Uncertainty and Profit*, Harper and Row, New York, 1965, p 233.

9   H S Becker, 'Notes on the concept of commitment', *American Journal of Sociology*, Vol 66, No 1, July 1960, pp 32-40.

10 See, for example, the section on defining and diagnosing illness, in E Freidson and J Lorber (Eds), *Medical Men and their Work*, op cit, pp 284-384.

11 S Cole and R Lejeune, 'Illness and the legitmation of failure', *American Sociological Review*, Vol 37, No 3, June 1972, p 352.

12 For a classic psychological approach to identity-stress, see E H Erikson, *Childhood and Society*, Norton, New York, 1950; also E H Erikson, *Identity, Youth and Crisis*, Norton, New York, 1968.

12

Redundancy and Stress

Steve Wood

Daniel and Mukerjee of the PEP group recently reviewed the *Strategies for Displaced Employees* that employees might use, and concluded that their development needs to be accompanied by extensive research. For 'Whilst there have been interesting and useful studies of closures and major lay-offs carried out in Britain...the volume in no way matches the importance of the problem'.(1)

Certainly the nature of these studies(2) has been limited. They have concentrated on manual and white-collar workers, and there has been a general neglect of managerial personnel. These studies have been grounded in the economists' theory of markets and have defined the redundancy problem as essentially one of labour mobility, as simply a problem of the redundant finding another job. Research has thus been concerned with how redundants fare in the labour market.

Recently there have been several attempts to direct research and policy away from economic analysis and towards, or at least to supplement it with, other disciplines of the social sciences.(3) The most detailed of such studies is that by Martin and Fryer. (4) They implicitly argue that it is not so much the quantity of research in the area of redundancy, but its quality that demands more studies are required. The study of redundancy requires what they term (following C W Mills) 'sociological imagination'. Their study is more than an account of what happened to a particular group of redundants; it embraces a detailed analysis of the social context in which it took place, including the attitudes of the redundants, and the managerial processes involved in the redundancy. One of the main justifications given by Martin and Fryer for their approach is that redundancy has 'non-economic' consequences. They are especially concerned to draw our attention to the psychological effects of redundancy and, in particular, to the stress that it causes. 'Redundancy is a time of stress, and sometimes distress, for all concerned'.(5)

Wedderburn(6), in her study of railwaymen, noted such psychological effects, which in extreme cases resulted in illness, or even suicides and deaths. Such cases may become part of the 'folklore' of the area in which the redundancy takes place; that is, Wedderburn tells us, regardless of whether there is any evidence that the deaths *were* caused by the redundancy or that there were other contributing factors. Wedderburn takes it for granted that redundancy does result in stress. She argues that these myths, which become part of the folklore, are themselves an indication of the stress which large-scale dismissals cause.

Given the assumed psychological effects of redundancy, it is not surprising that psychologists and behavioural scientists have also begun to look at the problem.(7) They have been the only writers who have explicitly discussed managers.* Such writers almost take it as inevitable that redundancy is a time of stress. Their main interest has been in devising new ways of helping managers, ways which are not simply financial, or directly concerned with helping the redundant to find a new job. It is believed that such help must concentrate on the redundant's strain for, as Harrison says, 'Help which does not recognise the depth and pervasiveness of the impact of (redundancy) must necessarily be superficial and quite possibly misguided.'(8)

Such help will be concerned to eliminate stress. It must focus on the redundant's *psychological* state. Writers advocating this type of help do not necessarily ignore the *social significance* of redundancy. Lehner, for example, states - unfortunately without specifying the illness he refers to - that redundancy contributes to 'the spreading disease within our society'.(9) By focusing on the redundant, writers such as Lehner do tend to take the society in which the redundancies occur as given.

In what follows, I shall attempt to show why writers see redundancy and stress as inevitably linked, and shall then briefly suggest that this conception causes them to limit the focus of their inquiry and reforms to stress elimination. Finally, I will also point to the way in which our thinking may be broadened.

THE CONCEPT OF STRESS

Does stress pertain to the situation or the individual? Rather than answer this question, we may

---

*There have been studies of managerial attitudes and ideology in which redundancy has been incorporated. They have, however, looked at it from the point of view of managers making people redundant rather than as something that happens to them.

distinguish between stressful situations and the individual state - stress or strain. In keeping with the terminology of some of the previous contributors to this book, the latter may be termed anxiety. It is perhaps also necessary to demarcate the anxiety from the behavioural responses to it. These distinctions are not always maintained in the literature on stress at work, and are often conflated. It may be argued that this is perhaps understandable, since it may not be possible to discuss and label anxiety and stress situations independently of each other. According to such thinking, anxiety can only be inferred from behavioural states, and stressful situations can only be defined by whether they induce anxiety. Thus, in a world of totally resilient people, there would be no way of identifying stress situations.

While this argument may be correct, it still begs the question of how we identify resilience; it may simply be seen as stating that in some senses the various distinctions that we have suggested are linked. They are indeed: they are linked by the 'theories' (common sense or otherwise) from which they derive. Stress does not identify itself, as it were, independently of such theories. It is, in fact, only identifiable if one knows what it would be *not* to be anxious or suffering from stress. That is, if one applies a standard specifying the 'natural' states of situations and individuals. Moreover, this criterion must be external, for neither the individual mental states nor the social situations studied can provide the standard, since they themselves are to be evaluated for their degree of stress.

The standard which is generally applied to specify the 'natural' condition of the individual in society involves a theory of human nature. In particular, man is viewed as having a wide range of creative potentialities whose self-realization exists as an inner necessity; such a need is capable of fulfilment in an industrial society in which men fulfil determinate functions in an organized system of work. Thus, the normal desirable position is for a man to be employed in a job. It is natural that men should seek work. Going to work, being in a job, is as natural as breathing. In the extreme form of this view, it is held that a man does not deserve to 'survive' if he is not in work and that a good conscientious worker can always find work.

Within this view, the manifestations of stress are taken to be routine, non-creative behaviours which are variously described, for example, as focusing on immediate consequences, restricting the number of alternative solutions to a problem and resisting change. This view underlies not only work specifically on stress, but also that of those writers on redundancy who have focused primarily on stress. Lehner, for example, writes

> Our western culture is a working culture, and achievement-oriented culture. If we do not work we have nothing to show for our time - whether in products, services, or satisfactions. If we do not work, we do not expect society to reward us.(10)

Lehner, like other writers, recognizes that there may be differences between jobs, ie not all jobs offer the same scope for, or type of self-fulfilment. Nevertheless, this does not affect these writers' views of the world, it simply points to another dimension of it. Society is not only organized around jobs, clusters of tasks, but it is also meritocratic, with equality of opportunity and personal liberty.

This points to a further important aspect of the dominant view of stress, namely that 'normal' individuals, while psychologically balanced, have different capacities to cope with challenging and, hence, potentially stressful situations. In other words, some people are more resilient than others. According to this argument, such challenging situations are seen as normal and the extent of their occurrence depends on where the individual is in the organized system of work. The higher up the system one goes, the more such stressful situations one has to confront. However, such circumstances only lead to stress in certain people, who cannot cope with, or live with stress. Thus, one man's stress is another man's challenge.

The view that the amount of responsibility and worry involved in the job increases as one goes up the hierarchy, and that only resilient people deserve, or can cope with the kinds of stress thought to be involved in top managerial life, is an important element in the legitimation of the differential pattern of rewards and the existing forms of organization in society. It is also this kind of thinking which leads professors to justify examinations by the fact that they are stressful situations; organizations to use stress-inducing techniques, such as T-Groups, to select personnel; and advertisers to exhort us all to 'relax' in our leisure time.* The extreme form of the resilient man is the entrepreneur who faces the challenge of satisfying men's needs by creatively producing and distributing goods. Such a man has been made the basis of a theory of economic development by McClelland.(11) He, in fact, posits that entrepreneurial attitudes towards risk taking, willingness to expend energy, willingness to innovate, and a readiness to make decisions and accept responsibility, arise out of a particular type of psychological need. This he terms the achievement need or n(eed for) achievement.

This view of man (or one very similar to it) lies behind much management thinking. A good example

---

*This is also the kind of thinking which leads firms to consider that management stress is the individual's and not the organization's responsibility, and also to favour 'hard' over 'soft' budgets for managers.

would be Mant's BIM report, *The Experienced Manager*. (12) In this, it is taken as given that men are (or at least ought to be, if only for their own good) ambitious, committed, mobile, willing, responsible, etc. The message is also clear that managers *need* to be flexible and resilient. While intelligence and education may form the basis of the vision of the meritocracy, they only provide a gateway to the managerial ranks. They have been supplemented as the 'currency' of the system by flexibility, character and psychological balance. Personality tests, T-Groups, intensive interviews all guarantee that it remains a meritocracy; 'elbowing', 'string pulling' and family connections are not required.

In Mant's report, inflexibility is seen to be at least partly independent of age and intelligence. There are cultural differences between the US and Britain. No assessment of these differences is made: it is largely taken, as in McClelland's thesis, that achievement-oriented people will be flexible and are a mark of a progressive 'mature' society, in which managers are professionals. A kind of development by contagion approach is suggested, ie we should have American-type business schools and management development programmes which will have the effect of making managers more flexible. In another BIM report, on redundancy, inflexibility is seen as related to security of tenure, and only indirectly with age and length of service. The report states:

> Managers' expectations that their present employment is secure increase with length of service.... Such managers appear to think they have acquired an 'established' status in the organization, regardless of their current or expected future contribution to the business. As a result, many of these managers are complacent and press less energetically to keep up to date.(13)

REDUNDANCY AND STRESS

From this brief, perhaps somewhat oversimplified account of the dominant view of stress, it can be seen why it seems 'natural' that redundancy and stress are linked. Firstly, a redundant may suffer from stress both because he may have a period without work (ie without behaving 'naturally') and because redundancy affects 'settled expectations'.

Given the belief that everybody is striving to get at least as far as they can, there is a second link between redundancy and stress. The redundancy itself may be thought to cause stress because it represents failure. It is the ultimate non-achievement, a step in the wrong direction, for human nature dictates that we want promotion, not demotion or redundancy.

It may be argued that such failure may be accepted with more resignation, given the belief in the rise of the meritocracy, since it may be seen as the result of a 'fair' process of selection. However, the argument is two-edged. Failure may be more unacceptable if accepting it means recognizing one's inferiority, either in terms of intelligence or flexibility. The belief in the existence of meritocracy serves, as Miliband says, 'to create the impression, not least amongst its victims, that social disadvantages are really a matter of personal, innate, God-given and insurmountable incapacity'.(14)

This points to a third connection between redundancy and stress. The redundant may be assumed to be suffering from stress not only as a result of the redundancy, but in order to have been selected to be made redundant in the first place. People who have failed, who are not resilient, dynamic, etc, are those who get made redundant. The BIM tells us that the complacent man, presses 'less energetically to keep up to date' and thus becomes 'vulnerable to redundancy'

From both BIM reports the lesson is clear: resilient men keep up to date and are likely to be the men making redundancies rather than being made redundant. If, however, redundancy becomes a possibility for them, they will 'see it coming' and 'get out' to greener pastures while the going's good. They won't wait around in declining industries, and will always want to 'get on' and perform 100% efficiently.

STRESS ELIMINATION AS THE SOLUTION TO THE REDUNDANCY PROBLEM

These three types of relations between redundancy and stress mean that stress elimination is given primacy over other definitions of the redundancy problem. The behavioural scientists offer a retrospective solution. Counselling and group work after the redundancy are recommended. The stress that results from a redundancy is often assumed to be of such intensity that the individual is unable to operate in the labour market, or, to use the terms of one writer who has stated this view, 'to think rationally about what to do to improve their situation'.(15) Pocock tells us that 'in practice this means first helping the person towards acceptance of his situation so that he can take responsibility for himself and gradually work towards a state of cautious optimism'.(16)

These retrospective measures are also required because redundancy is linked to failure. The redundant is defined as a *deviant* man and, as such, is in need of treatment. The redundant has failed to keep himself 'fit' for the market economy. He is either directly or indirectly labelled as a 'rotten apple', 'a piece of dead wood' who has to be 'shaken out' or, to be less pejorative, 'obsolete'. The redundant must be made resilient in order to make himself marketable. The redundancy may thus be seen as challenging the manager to shake himself out of his complacency, to be what organizations want, ie flexible.

The BIM seem to favour a more preventive form of stress elimination, that may be termed the *management development* solution to redundancy. While firms are encouraged to help in this, the onus is firmly placed on the individual manager:

> 'Managers must recognise and accept a personal responsibility for the planning and evolution of their own careers throughout their working lives'.(17)

Since it is job security that has led to complacency and inflexibility, the manager must be encouraged to be mobile, or at least oriented towards mobility. He must become as mobile as capital, such that, instead of getting himself into a position where he becomes a reluctant redundant, he must be a kind of voluntary 'casual' manager. Such a man is continually asking himself, 'Can I get another job outside my present one?' and if the answer is 'No', he does his own management development. The totally resourceful manager is continually developing - management development becomes a dialectic on his own activities and progress. He can thus, somewhat automatically, move in an instance almost anywhere. His job security is provided by his marketability, which is his flexibility (and since they are seen as going hand in hand, his 'mobile orientation'). Indeed, to the resourceful manager, the mobility achieved through flexibility represents the ultimate or prime reward in life. Job security is only associated with job stability or sticking with one firm for life, by old-fashioned 'non-professional' managers, or Mant's 'backbone managers'. The BIM argue that the very occurrence of redundancies serves to show how misguided are managers who do not 'press... energetically to keep up to date', and how unrealistic are their ideologies concerning security of employment.

I shall now briefly outline some major difficulties in the kind of thinking we have just described, and emphasize those which provide clues for more fruitful and less limited approaches. Firstly, redundancy is assumed to be inevitable, and treated as non-problematic; thus the *problem of redundancy is simply the problem of the redundant*. In this way, it represents no break from the dominant economic tradition in the study of redundancy. The fundamental problem is that of the redundant finding an alternative job. Acceptance of the redundancy is not taken to be accepting the right to be made redundant (for this is taken as given) but simply accepting that he must find another job, and rationally thinking about what he has to offer the market and community. This kind of argument completely ignores the possibility that, for the employee, the rational thing is not to accept the redundancy, since, by definition, accepting redundancy is to accept the necessity of being mobile. Under the management development solution, it is assumed that man is rational enough, or at least eventually will be, to be in a permanent state of readiness to leave; thus there is no *real* redundancy problem since he is always 'fit' to 'take on' the market.

To contest the redundancy is seen, both by managers making the redundancies and by any outside aid that they may enlist to counsel and help the redundant, as further validation of the redundant's right to be dismissed. The unwillingness to admit of stress or of the need for help is taken as a sign of being a difficult, or deteriorating case. If the redundant disputes the assessment of his performance on which the redundancy decision is based, this is also an indication of his state. The modern resourceful manager should know how he is getting on and adjust his performance accordingly. Thus, appeals to the effect that the firm should have forewarned the redundant about his likely future are simply seen as 'sour grapes', or indicators of the redundant's inability to help himself, and that he is thus not the kind of man the firm wants, or even that it 'ought' to employ.

Moreover, by largely attributing redundancy to the

manager's failure to remain flexible and resilient, reports such as the BIM's, *underplay the possible inevitability of redundancies because of what the Institute terms 'outside factors'*, ie factors over which the manager has no control. This has several consequences. Firstly, it neglects the fact that it is not the redundant who labels or defines himself as inflexible and obsolete. Indeed, as Professor Morris has stated, managers may be 'thought of as dead wood and yet still feel very much alive and responsible for a home and family'. It is, indeed, certain managers *qua* definers acting in the interests of the firm who label certain personnel obsolete, inefficient and so on. Such definitions may be used as a way of avoiding arbitrariness and favouritism in the selection of redundants. Furthermore, it is often a convenient mode of solving what might be termed the management succession problem in reverse, the problem of career blockage. It is easy to accommodate the assumed ambitions of younger managers in expanding organizations, but with economic pressures the older, blocking man must be bumped. There is, of course, nothing inherent in a man's behaviour that he should be labelled as obsolete, tense, inflexible or resistant to change. It depends on an underlying evaluation of whether he is being positive (productive) or negative (unproductive).(18) Labels such as 'dead wood' may thus be seen as representing, to use C W Mills' phrase,(19) *'vocabularies of motive'* used to make sense of differentiations and classifications already made, and to justify the need for certain men to move over for others.

A second consequence of this is that, underlying the dominant model, is the view that not only are there always jobs available for conscientious people and, thus, at least in the long run, managers will be unaffected by having been made redundant, but that, in fact, the redundant will be a better man for having been made redundant. That is, for having been presented with a challenge. The remedial procedures are then justified and determined by this concept of adaptive failure, and the assumption that the organization has not contributed to the redundant's problem. The stress-elimination techniques may guarantee that the redundant sees that it is he who must be adapted (or better still adapt himself), not the situation from which he has been rejected, as well as the one to which he is preparing or, at least trying, to enter.

A third and related consequence is that, although the techniques of stress elimination may guarantee that any 'chip on the shoulder' the redundant may develop is seen as unjustified, and that any bitterness is channelled into himself, ie they may 'cool him out', such techniques may not, in fact, eliminate stress. There is a danger that they may even amplify stress. This is so, not simply because certain techniques such as T-Groups and creativity blocks may induce stress without eliminating it,(20) but also because they serve to define the redundant as requiring treatment. Attributing redundancy to personal failings may mask perhaps a more important reason why supportive groups and education programmes for redundants may at the present time be relevant, as well as the importance of what Harrison terms the information and administrative aspects of redundancy. That is even if the redundant accepts the redundancy as a fact of life which in no way reflects on him, stress may develop because of uncertainty about the norms and operation of the labour market.

It seems to me that it is at least partly because job security has been the norm for managers and hence the redundant lacks norms concerning job search and the labour market, that redundancy presents a problem. It seems at least as appropriate to view redundancy as a change in the norms of managerial employment, as it does to see it as proof that managers have always failed to be realistic and resourceful. Managers can now, like workers, lose their job through no fault of their own.* (It might be 'better' if managers admitted this more readily, instead of disguising it with concepts such as failure and dead wood.)

Behavioural scientists may argue that their techniques are appropriate for all kinds of psychological stress. But are they? They may be based on entirely different values from those appropriate for helping the redundant to find a job in what Morris terms the mainstream. Such techniques are concerned to draw out the manager's achievement and creativity needs; that is, they are concerned with entrepreneurship. Such needs may be associated with what have been termed 'subterranean' as opposed to the 'formal work values' or the 'protestant ethic' required in the kind of hierarchical and formalized system of modern industry. Does it really help the 'typical' redundant manager to think of transforming his hobbies into commercial ventures, setting up his own business, finding something in the highlands of Scotland, or to become a ruthless, highly mobile 'wheeler-dealer'? Pahl and Pahl(21) draw our attention to the fact that writers such as McClelland and Mant do not face up to the problems of what would happen if everybody behaved as entrepreneurs, as active movers, measuring their success by the speed of their mobility, etc.

Another difficulty in the dominant view of stress is that it implies that, if it does occur, it does so because the individual has been alien to his 'true' self, ie inflexible and complacent. This need not be the case. Even if the redundant perceives himself to have failed, his 'authentic' aims may not involve striving for success. He may accept the existence of the meritocracy but adopt a strategy which is somewhat opposite to striving for success, namely, striving to avoid failure. This is the kind of thing that Pahl and Pahl discovered among some of the managers they studied: 'Very often it is the fear of falling rather than the positive aspiration to climb that pushes...men on.'(22)

---

*It is largely because redundancy may signify the possibility of losing one's job through no fault of one's own that the study of the direct effects of redundancy on stayers, as opposed to redundants, becomes relevant.

By treating, as do Pahl and Pahl, manager's orientations to 'success' and 'career' as problematic, we may open up fresh approaches to the problem of managerial manpower allocation, even within hierarchical organizations.

To be more general, the main trouble with the dominant view of stress is that, although it may be said to pinpoint the central ills of capitalism - unemployment, immobility, inflexibility, the effects of the association of personal security with job security - it characterizes them as abnormal. This procedure tends to hinder any full-scale investigation of their causes (which are assumed not to be endemic). They are to be explained by man's not behaving 'naturally', the solution is then to rid man of his 'alien' state. Thus, what at first sight looks like a major critique of society (or at least its 'diseases'), ends up by taking the existing society for granted and failing even to consider anxiety or stress as a consequence of the social and economic order. It has been noted that this is a danger inherent in all psychologism:

> To bestow some sort of higher ontological status upon psychological consequences is *ipso facto* a symptom of the mis- or non-apprehension of the social process that produced them.'(23)

Analysis of the redundancy problem must examine the social and economic conditions that produce redundancy and the problems associated with it. I shall briefly illustrate this by reference to the BIM's definition of redundancy, as the problem of immobile personnel. As we have seen, they largely treat this as a psychological propensity inherent in managers. We must, however, consider whether this reflects the institutional arrangements of society. That is, we must consider whether, in fact, individuals have the right to quit particular jobs and organizations.

The BIM admit that existing pension schemes inhibit mobility. Numerous other such constraints could be named, such that in no sense could it be said that the individual has the right to quit. It is, for example, very difficult if not impossible, to move from one professional field of work to another because most occupational groups demand commitment at an early age. One must not forget even more subtle constraints on mobility, such as the notion that a person who changes jobs regularly is unstable and not a good risk for employment.

If immobility is seen as at least an element in the redundancy problem, the answer lies in changing our institutions. As Roth has recently stated:

> Instead of trying to arrange things to discourage turnover and to force people to stick to a certain pattern of life and to given memberships and relations whether they want to or not, we should instead seek to structure our social organization to facilitate the right to quit - the right to quit one's job, profession, country, institution, ideology, spouse, parents and, in fact, life itself.(24)

This will require considerable change. For example, setting entry requirements to occupations which are as easy as possible for all reasonably competent people, rather than placing as many restrictions as possible in their way. Pension plans must have as their unit of coverage not a given company, occupation or industry, but the entire country - and eventually the world.

The emphasis should be on institutions, and only indirectly on psychological states. In short, we must get away from enterprise-oriented thinking and institutions. The extent to which this can be achieved in capitalism is an open question. Its achievement will depend on coupling the narrower problem of employment relations with the broader organizational design questions. It must be based on assuming that organizational structures have some autonomy from the economy, and that there are no

'natural laws of techniques' such that events, like the increasing size of units of production and its associated growth in hierarchical organization, are inherently 'necessary'. The hierarchical notion of the organization underlies the unitary view of career progression, so much a part of current thinking, and on which our notions of success and failure depend. The researcher must not simply design *de novo* non-hierarchical organizations with no regard for existing arrangements. Investigations of at least the depth of Martin and Fryer's are required.*
Rather than simply taking as given (as does the dominant view of stress outlined above) the association of job security with personal security, we must examine the mechanisms which produce this. We must consider what it is about the organization as a social arrangement that creates for the individual the sort of order in which he can experience life as being secure. It has not been my intention to discuss job security in these terms. But, clearly, views which see security - personal or job - as the effect of psychological dispositions, as well as panaceas such as welfare corporatism, take the important processes as given.

References

1   W W Daniel and S Mukerjee, 'Strategies for displaced employees', *PEP Broadsheet*, Vol 38, No 517, January 1970, p 56.

2   The most recent of such studies include, M I A Bulmer, 'Mining redundancy: a case study of the workings of the Redundancy Payments Act in the Durham coalfield', *Industrial Relations Journal*, Vol 2, No 4, Winter 1971, pp 3-21; W W Daniel, 'Whatever happened to the workers in Woolwich?' *PEP Broadsheet*, Vol 38, No 537, July 1972; F Herron, 'Redundancy and Redevelopment from UCS 1969-71', *Scottish Journal of Political Economy*,

---

*Such research may also point to alternatives to redundancy, within existing organizational arrangements.

Vol 19, No 3, November 1972, pp 231-51;
D I MacKay, I Boddy, J Brack, J A Drack, N Jones,
Labour Markets under Different Employment Conditions,
George Allen and Unwin, 1970; D I MacKay, *After
the Shakeout*, Oxford Economic Papers (NS), Vol 24,
No 1, March 1972, pp 82-110; D I MacKay and G L
Reid, 'Redundancy, unemployment and manpower
policy', *Economic Journal*, Vol 82, No 328,
December 1972, pp 1256-72; G L Reid, 'The role of
the employment service in redeployment', *British
Journal of Industrial Relations*, Vol 9, No 2,
July 1971, pp 160-81.

3   Peter Seglow, 'Reactions to redundancy: the
influence of the work situation', *Industrial
Relations Journal*, Vol 1, No 2, September 1970,
pp 7-22; Brenda Thomas and C Madigan, 'Strategy
and job choice after redundancy: a case study in
the aircraft industry', *Sociological Review*,
Vol 22, No 1, February 1974, pp 83-102; Michael
Mann, *Workers on the Move*, Cambridge University
Press, 1973; R Martin and R H Fryer, 'Management
and redundancy; an analysis of planned
organizational change', *British Journal of
Industrial Relations*, Vol 8, No 1, March 1970,
pp 69-84.

4   R Martin and R H Fryer, *Redundancy and Paternalist
Capitalism*, George Allen and Unwin, 1973.

5   ibid, p 187.

6   D Wedderburn, *Redundancy and the Railwaymen*,
Cambridge University Press, 1965, p 150.

7   See, for example, R Harrison, 'Towards a strategy
for helping redundant and retiring managers',
Management Education and Development, Vol 4,
Part (2), August 1973, pp 73-85; G Lehner, 'How
to manage the victims of a cutback', *Innovation*,
Vol 21, 1971, pp 42-7; P Pocock, 'Softening the
Blow of Redundancy', *Personnel Management*, Vol 4,
No 6, June 1972, pp 25-7.

8   R Harrison, ibid, p 77.

9   G Lehner, op cit, p 42.

10 ibid, p 43.

11 D C McClelland, *The Acheiving Society*, Van Nostrand, Princeton, NJ, 1961.

12 A Mant, *The Experienced Manager*, BIM, 1969. For a brief critique of this, see J M and R E Pahl, *Managers and Their Wives*, Allen Lane, 1972, pp 34-8.

13 BIM, *Managerial Mobility and Redundancy*, 1972, p 11.

14 R Miliband, *The State in Capitalist Society*, Quartet Books, 1973, p 216.

15 R Harrison, op cit, p 79.

16 P Pocock, op cit, p 27.

17 BIM, op cit, p 4.

18 See Erich Fromm, *Man for Himself*, Routledge and Kegan Paul, 1948, especially pp 50-117. He shows that the same behaviour may be evaluated positively or negatively, eg 'inert' is the negative equivalent of the positive form 'composed under stress', and 'inconsistent' is the negative of able to change.

19 C W Mills, 'Situated actions and vocabularies of motive', in C W Mills, *Power, Politics and People*, Oxford University Press, New York, 1963, pp 439-52.

20 The 'experimental' evidence on stress inducement in laboratory situations is not very conclusive. See E E Levitt, *The Psychology of Anxiety*, Paladin, 1971, pp 102-116. There are similar doubts about the validity of encounter and T-Groups. See, for example, J P Ward, 'The T-Group', *Encounter*, Vol XLll, No 3, March 1974, pp 30-40; M A Lieberman, I D Yalom and M B Miles, 'The

impact of encounter groups on participants: some preliminary findings', *Journal of Applied Behavioral Science*, Vol 1, January - February 1972, pp 29-50; C Argyris, 'Do personal growth laboratories represent an alternative culture?', *Journal of Applied Behavioral Science*, Vol 8, No 1, January - February 1972, pp 7-28.

21 J M and R E Pahl, op cit, p 38.

22 ibid, p 259.

23 P L Berger and H Kellner, 'Marriage and the construction of reality: An exercise in the microsociology of knowledge', in B Cosin, *et al*, *School and Society: A Sociological Reader*, Routledge and Kegan Paul in association with The Open University Press, 1971, pp 23-31.

24 J Roth, 'The right to quit', *Sociological Review*, (NS) Vol 21, No 3, August 1973, pp 381-96.

Bibliography

C Argyris, *Understanding Organizational Behaviour*, Dorsey, Homewood, Ill., 1960.

C Argyris, 'Today's problems with tomorrow's organizations', *Journal of Management Studies*, Vol 4, No 1, February 1967, pp 31-55.

C Argyris, 'Do personal growth laboratories represent an alternative culture?', *Journal of Applied Behavioral Science*, Vol 8, No 1, January - February 1972, pp 7-28.

H S Becker, 'Notes on the concept of commitment', *American Journal of Sociology*, Vol 66, No 1, July 1960, pp 32-40.

H S Becker and A Strauss, 'Careers, Personality and Adult Socialization', in H S Becker (ed), *Sociological Work*, Allen Lane, 1971.

S Beer, *Decision and Control*, Wiley, New York, 1966.

S Benet, *Abkhasians, The Long-Living People of the Caucasus*, Holt, Rinehart and Winston, New York, 1974.

W G Bennis, 'Beyond bureaucracy', in W G Bennis and P E Slater, *The Temporary Society*, Harper and Row, New York, 1968.

J Bensman and I Gerver, 'Crime and punishment in the factory: the function of deviancy in maintaining the social system', *American Sociological Review*, Vol 28, No 4, December 1963, pp 588-98.

P L Berger and H Kellner, 'Marriage and the construction of reality. An exercise in the microsociology of knowledge', in B Cosin, *et al, School and Society: A Sociological Reader*, Routledge and Kegan Paul in association with The Open University Press, 1971, pp 23-31.

H P Beynon, *Working for Ford*, Penguin, 1973.

R Blake and J S Mouton, *The Managerial Grid*, Gulf Publishing, Houston, 1964.

R O Blood and D M Wolfe, *Husbands and Wives: The Dynamics of Family Living*, Free Press of Glencoe and Collier-Macmillan, New York, 1960.

J Boissevain, *Friends of Friends - Networks Manipulators and Coalitions*, Basil Blackwell, 1974.

E Bott, *Family and Social Network*, Tavistock, 1957.

R Boudon, *The Uses of Structuralism*, Heinemann Educational Books, 1971.

J V Brady, 'Ulcers in the "executive" monkeys', *Scientific American*, Vol 199, 1958, pp 95-100.

H C Bredemeier and R M Stephenson, *The Analysis of Social Systems*, Holt, Rinehart and Winston, New York, 1962.

BIM, *Managerial Mobility and Redundancy*, 1972.

P L Broadhurst, 'Emotionality and the Yerkes-Dodson Law', *Journal of Experimental Psychology*, Vol 54, 1957, pp 345-52.

U Bronfenbrenner, *Two Worlds of Childhood: USA and USSR*, George Allen and Unwin, 1971.

V E Buck, *Working Under Pressure*, Staples Press, 1972.

M I A Bulmer, 'Mining redundancy: a case study of the workings of the Redundancy Payments Act in the Durham coalfield', *Industrial Relations Journal*, Vol 2, Winter 1971, pp 3-21.

S Cole and R Lejeune, 'Illness and the legitimation of failure, *American Sociological Review*, Vol 37, June 1972, pp 347-56.

R Coser, 'Evasiveness as a response to structural ambivalence', *Social Science and Medicine*, Vol 1, 1967, pp 203-18.

S Cotgrove, J Dunham and C Vamplew, *The Nylon Spinners: A Case Study in Productivity Bargaining and Job Enlargement*, George Allen and Unwin, 1971.

R M Cyert and J G March, *A Behavioral Theory of The Firm*, Prentice-Hall, Englewood Cliffs, NJ, 1963.

M Dalton, 'Conflicts between staff and line managerial officers', *American Sociological Review*, Vol 15, 1950, pp 342-51.

M Dalton, *Men Who Manage: Fusions of Feeling and Theory in Administration*, Wiley, New York, 1959.

W W Daniel and S Mukerjee, 'Strategies for displaced

employees', *PEP Broadsheet*, Vol 36, No 517, January 1970.

W W Daniel, 'Whatever happened to the workers in Woolwich?', *PEP Broadsheet*, Vol 38, No 537, July 1972.

N G Davey, *The External Consultant's Role in Organizational Change*, Michigan State University Press, East Lansing, Michigan, 1971.

F Davis, 'Uncertainty in medical prognosis, clinical and functional', in E Freidson and J Lorber (eds), *Medical Men and Their Work*, Aldine-Atherton, Chicago, 1972.

S Dinitz, R R Dynes and A C Clarke, *Deviance: Studies in the Process of Stigmatization and Societal Reaction*, Oxford University Press, 1969.

P F Drucker, *The Practice of Management*, Mercury Books, 1961. (First published by Heinemann, 1955.)

F E Emery and E L Trist, 'The causal texture of organizational environments', *Human Relations*, Vol 18, No 1, February 1965, pp 21-32.

E H Erikson, *Childhood and Society*, Norton, New York, 1950.

E H Erikson, *Identity, Youth and Crisis*, Norton, New York, 1968.

L Festinger, *A Theory of Cognitive Dissonance*, Row, Peterson, New York, 1957.

F E Fiedler, *A Theory of Leadership Effectiveness*, McGraw-Hill, New York, 1967.

A Flanders, *The Fawley Productivity Agreements: A Case Study of Management and Collective Bargaining*, Faber, 1964.

R Fletcher, *Family and Marriage in Britain*, revised edition, Penguin, 1966.

M P Fogarty, R Rapoport and R N Rapoport, *Sex, Career and Family*, PEP and George Allen and Unwin, 1971.

M Fortes, 'Ritual and office in tribal society', in M Gluckman (ed), *Essays on the Ritual of Social Relations*, Manchester University Press, 1962, pp 53-88.

R Frankenburg, *Village on the Border*, Cohen and West, 1957.

E Freidson and J Lorber (eds), *Medical Men and Their Work*, Aldine-Atherton, Chicago, 1972.

E Fromm, *Man for Himself*, Routledge and Kegan Paul, 1948.

E Goffman, *Asylums: Essays on the Social Situation of Mental Patients and Other Inmates*, Pelican, 1971.

J Goody (ed), *Succession to High Office*, Cambridge Papers in Social Anthropology, No 4, Cambridge University Press, 1966.

A W Gouldner, *Patterns of Industrial Bureaucracy*, Free Press of Glencoe, New York, 1954.

A W Gouldner, 'Cosmopolitans and locals: towards an analysis of latent social roles, I, II', *Administrative Science Quarterly*, Vol 2, 3, 1957-8, pp 281-306; No 4, 1957-8, pp 444-80.

D Gowler and K Legge, 'Occupational role development - Parts 1 and 2', *Personnel Review*, Vol 1, Spring and Summer 1972, pp 12-27, pp 58-73.

L E Greiner, 'Patterns of organizational change', in G W Dalton and P R Lawrence (with the collaboration of L E Greiner), (eds), *Organizational Change and Development*, Irwin, Homewood, Ill., 1970.

J A Hammes, 'Visual discrimination learning as a function of shock, fear and task difficulty', *Journal of Comparative Neurology and Psychology*,

Vol 49, 1956, pp 481-4.

R Harrison, 'Towards a strategy for helping redundant and retiring managers', *Management Education and Development*, Vol 4, Part 2, August 1973, pp 73-85.

F A Heller, *Managerial Decision-Making*, Tavistock, 1971.

F Herron, 'Redundancy and redevelopment from UCS 1969-71', *Scottish Journal of Political Economy*, Vol 19, No 2, November 1972, pp 231-51.

P Hill, *Towards a New Philosophy of Management, The Company Development Programme of Shell UK Ltd*, Gower Press, 1971.

J W Humble, *Improving Management Performance*, Management Publications, BIM, 1960.

E Jaques, *The Changing Culture of a Factory*, Tavistock, 1951.

E Jaques, *Equitable Payment*, Heinemann Educational Books, 1961.

G N Jones, *Planned Organizational Change: A Study in Change Dynamics*, Routledge and Kegan Paul, 1968.

R L Kahn, D M Wolfe, R P Quinn, J D Snoek and R A Rosenthal, *Organizational Stress: Studies in Role Conflict and Ambiguity*, Wiley, New York, 1964.

E Knight, *Risk, Uncertainty and Profit*, Harper and Row, New York, 1965.

K E Knight, 'A descriptive model of the intra-firm innovation process', *Journal of Business*, Vol 40, October 1967, pp 478-96.

P R Lawrence and J W Lorsch, *Organization and Environment: Managing Differentiation and Integration*, Harvard University Press, Cambridge, Mass., 1967.

P R Lawrence and J W Lorsch, 'New management job: the integrator', *Harvard Business Review*, Vol 46, No 6, November - December 1967, pp 142-51.

G Lehner, 'How to manage the victims of a cutback', *Innovation*, Vol 21, 1971, pp 42-7.

E M Lemert, 'The concept of secondary deviation', in E M Lemert, *Human Deviance, Social Problems and Social Control*, Prentice-Hall, Englewood Cliffs, NJ, 1967, pp 49-52.

E E Levitt, *The Psychology of Anxiety*, Paladin, 1971. (First published by Bobbs-Merrill, New York, 1967).

M A Lieberman, I D Yalom and M B Miles, 'The impact of encounter groups on participants: some preliminary findings', *Journal of Applied Behavioral Science*, Vol 8, No 1, January - February 1972, pp 29-50.

R Likert, *The Human Organization*, McGraw-Hill, New York, 1967.

A E Lowe and R W Shawe, 'An analysis of managerial biasing: evidence from a company's budgeting process', *Journal of Management Studies*, Vol 5, No 3, October 1968, pp 304-15.

T Lupton and D Gowler, 'Selecting a Wage Payment System', *Research Paper No 3*, Engineering Employers' Federation, 1969.

D I MacKay, I Boddy, J Brack, J A Drack and N Jones, *Labour Markets Under Different Employment Conditions*, George Allen and Unwin, 1970.

D I MacKay, 'After the Shake-Out', *Oxford Economic Papers* (NS), Vol 24, No 1, March 1972, pp 82-110.

D I MacKay and G L Reid, 'Redundancy, unemployment and manpower policy', *Economic Journal*, Vol 82, No 328, December 1972, pp 1256-72.

M Mann, *Workers on the Move*, Cambridge University Press, 1973.

A Mant, *The Experienced Manager*, BIM, 1969.

R Martin and R H Fryer, 'Management and redundancy: an analysis of planned organizational change', *British Journal of Industrial Relations*, Vol 8, No 1, March 1970, pp 69-84.

R Martin and R H Fryer, *Redundancy and Paternalist Capitalism*, George Allen and Unwin, 1973.

D C McClelland, *The Acheiving Society*, Van Nostrand, Princeton, NJ, 1961.

D McGregor, *The Human Side of Enterprise*, McGraw-Hill, New York, 1960.

D McGregor, *The Professional Manager*, McGraw-Hill, New York, 1967.

McKinsey Associates, 'Unlocking the computer's profit potential', *McKinsey Quarterly*, Vol 5, No 2, 1968.

D Mechanic, *Medical Sociology, A Selective View*, Free Press of Glencoe, New York, 1968.

S Melman, *Decision-Making and Productivity*, Wiley, New York, 1958.

R K Merton, *Social Theory and Social Structure*, Free Press of Glencoe, New York, 1949.

R K Merton, 'Patterns of Influence, Local and Cosmopolitan Influentials', in R K Merton, *Social Theory and Social Structure*, Free Press of Glencoe, New York, 1949.

R K Merton, 'The role-set: problems in sociological theory, *British Journal of Sociology*, Vol 8, No 2, June 1957, pp 106-20.

R Miliband, *The State in Capitalist Society*, Quartet Books, 1973.

C W Mills, 'Situated actions and vocabularies of motive', in C W Mills, *Power, Politics and People*, Oxford University Press, New York, 1963, pp 439-52.

C F Molander, 'Management by objectives in perspective' *Journal of Management Studies*, Vol 9, No 1, February 1972, pp 74-81.

J F Morris, 'Three Aspects of the Person in Social Life', in R Ruddock (ed), *Six Approaches to the Person*, Routledge and Kegan Paul, 1972.

J Morris and J G Burgoyne, *Developing Resourceful Managers*, Institute of Personnel Management, 1973.

J J Morse and J W Lorsch, 'Beyond theory Y', *Harvard Business Review*, Vol 48, No 3, May - June 1970, pp 61-8.

E Mumford, *Job Satisfaction, A Study of Computer Specialists*, Longman, 1972.

S F Nadel, *The Theory of Social Structure*, Cohen and West, 1957.

V Olesen and E Whittaker, 'Adjudication of student awareness in professional socialization: the language of laughter and silence', *Sociological Quarterly*, Vol 7, No 3, Summer 1965, pp 381-96.

J M and R E Pahl, *Managers and Their Wives*, Allen Lane, 1971..

A Pettigrew, *The Politics of Organizational Decision-Making*, Tavistock, 1973.

P Pocock, 'Softening the blow of redundancy', *Personnel Management*, Vol 4, No 6, June 1972, pp 25-7.

R and R Rapoport, *Dual-career Families*, Penguin, 1971.

G L Reid, 'The role of the employment service in redeployment', *British Journal of Industrial Relations*, Vol 9, No 2, July 1971, pp 160-81.

W H Reid, 'Upward communication in industrial hierarchies', *Human Relations*, Vol 15, No 1, February 1962, pp 1-15.

G Ritzer and H M Trice, *An Occupation in Conflict - A Study of the Personnel Manager*, Cornell University Press, Ithaca, NY, 1969.

E M Rogers and F Floyd Shoemaker, *Communication of Innovations, A Cross-cultural Approach*, Free Press of Glencoe, New York, 1971. (First edition of this book, by E M Rogers, was published as *Diffusion of Innovations*, Free Press of Glencoe, 1962).

J Roth, 'The right to quit', *Sociological Review*, (NS) Vol 21, No 3, August 1973, pp 381-96.

R Ruddock (ed), *Six Approaches to the Person*, Routledge and Kegan Paul, 1972.

L R Sayles, *Managerial Behavior: Administration in Complex Organizations*, McGraw-Hill, New York, 1964.

E H Schein, *Process Consultation: Its Role in Organization Development*, Addison-Wesley, Reading, Mass., 1969.

W R Scott, *Social Processes and Social Structures*, Holt, Rinehart and Winston, New York, 1970.

P Seglow, 'Reactions to redundancy: the influence of the work situation', *Industrial Relations Journal*, Vol 1, No 2, September 1970, pp 7-22.

H A Simon, 'Rational choice and the structure of the environment', *Psychological Review*, Vol 63, No 2, March 1956, pp 129-39.

C Sofer, *The Organization From Within: A Comparative*

Study of Social Institutions Based on a Sociotherapeutic Approach, Tavistock, 1961.

A Strauss, 'Transformations of identity', in A Rose (ed), *Human Behaviour and Social Processes,* Routledge and Kegan Paul, 1971.

B Thomas and C Madigan, 'Strategy and job choice after redundancy: a case study in the aircraft industry', *Sociological Review,* Vol 22, No 1, February 1974, pp 83-102.

A Toffler, *Future Shock,* Bodley Head, 1970.

G Turner, *The Car Makers,* Eyre and Spottiswoode, 1963.

V H Vroom and P W Yetton, *Leadership and Decision-Making,* University of Pittsburgh Press, Pittsburgh, 1973.

J P Ward, 'The T-Group', *Encounter,* Vol XLII, No 3, 1974, pp 30-40.

M Weber, *The Theory of Social and Economic Organization,* Free Press of Glencoe, New York, 1964. (Translated by A M Henderson and T Parsons, Oxford University Press, New York, 1947).

D Wedderburn, *Redundancy and the Railwaymen,* Cambridge University Press, 1965.

J D Wickens, 'Management by Objectives - an appraisal', *Journal of Management Studies,* Vol 5, No 3, October 1968, pp 365-79.

R M Yerkes and J D Dodson, 'The relation of strength of stimulus to rapidity of habit-formation', *Journal of Comparative Neurology and Psychology,* Vol 18, 1908, pp 459-82.

P W Yetton, *Participation and Leadership Style: A Descriptive Model of a Manager's Choice of a Decision Process,* doctoral thesis, Carnegie-Mellon University, 1972.

M Young and P Willmott, *Family and Kinship in East London*, Routledge and Kegan Paul, 1957.

M Young and P Willmott, *The Symmetrical Family: A Study of Work and Leisure in the London Region*, Routledge and Kegan Paul, 1973.

NAME INDEX

Argyris, C.   69, 109-10, 114, 137, 209

Becker, H.S.   180, 186, 188, 189
Beer, S.   128, 132
Benet, S.   17
Bennis, W.G.   105, 106, 114
Bensman, J.   170, 178
Berger, P.L.   209
Beynon, H.P.   178
Blake, R.   101
Blood, R.O.   86
Boddy, I.   207
Boissevain, J.   50
Bott, E.   85
Boudon, R.   163
Brack, J.   207
Brady, J.V.   28, 33
Bredemeier, H.C.   163
Brien, C.M.   ix
Broadhurst, P.L.   27, 33
Bronfenbrenner, U.   17
Buck, V.E.   50, 68
Bulmer, M.I.A.   206
Burgoyne, J.G.   x, xi, 3, 4, 5, 6, 7, 69
Butterworth, J.   178

Clarke, A.C.   178
Cole, S.   189
Coser, R.   181, 189
Cotgrove, S.   150
Cyert, R.M.   50

Dalton, M.   69, 150, 178
Daniel, W.W.   190, 206
Davey, N.G.   150
Davis, F.   181, 189
Dinitz, S.   178
Dodson, J.D.   27

Donaldson, J.   xi, 4, 6, 9
Drack, J.A.   207
Drucker, P.F.   50
Dunham, J.   150
Dynes, R.R.   178

Eccles, A.   178
Emery, F.E.   132
Erikson, E.H.   189

Fairhurst, E.   xi, 3, 4, 14, 189
Festinger, L.   51
Fiedler, F.E.   90, 101
Flanders, A.   149
Fletcher, R.   85, 86
Fogarty, M.P.   86
Fortes, M.   164
Frankenburg, R.   17
Freidson, E.   189
Fromm, E.   208
Fryer, M.   191, 206, 207

Gerver, I.   170, 178
Gluckman, M.   164
Goffman, E.   188
Goody, J.   164
Gouldner, A.W.   69, 164
Gowler, D.   x, 3, 4, 6, 7, 9, 11, 51, 114, 178
Greiner, L.E.   150

Hammes, J.A.   27, 33
Harrison, R.   192, 202, 207, 208
Heller, F.   90, 101
Herron, F.   206
Herzberg, F.   175
Hill, P.   150
Humble, J.W.   50

Jacques, E.   8, 149, 150
Jones, G.N.   149
Jones, N.   207

Kahn, R.L.   43, 49, 50, 68, 121, 132
Kellner, H.   209
Knight, E.   183, 189
Knight, K.E.   116, 132

Lawrence, P.R.   68, 106, 114, 131, 150
Legge, K.   x, 3, 4, 6, 7, 11, 51, 178
Lehner, G.   192, 194, 207
Lejeune, R.   189
Lemert, E.M.   170, 178
Levitt, E.E.   49, 68, 208
Liebermann, M.A.   208
Likert, R.   101
Lloyd, P.   ix
Lorber, J.   189
Lorsch, J.W.   68, 114, 131
Lowe, E.A.   163
Lupton, T.   xi, xii, 3, 4, 12, 13, 114, 178
Lynton, R.P.   126

MacKay, D.I.   207
Madigan, C.   207
Mann, M.   207
Mant, A.   196, 199, 203, 208
March, J.G.   50
Martin, R.   191, 206, 207
Maslow, A.H.   175
McClelland, D.C.   50, 195, 196, 203, 208
McGregor, D.   101, 103, 114
McKinsey Associates,   119, 132
Mechanic, D.   1, 8, 17
Melman, S.   121, 132
Merton, R.K.   48, 49, 50, 68, 69
Miles, M.B.   208
Miliband, R.   197, 208
Mills, C.W.   191, 201, 208

224

Molander, C.F.   163
Morris, J.F.   xii, 4, 7, 33, 49, 69, 201, 203
Morse, J.J.   106, 114
Mouton, J.S.   101
Mukerjee, S.   190, 206
Mumford, E.   xii, 4, 10, 114, 132

Nadel, S.F.   17, 49
North Paul,   175

Olesen, V.   181, 189

Pahl, J.M.   85, 203, 204, 208, 209
Pahl, R.E.   85, 203, 204, 208, 209
Pettigrew, A.   125, 126, 127, 132
Pocock, P.   198, 207, 208

Quinn, R.P.   49, 68, 132

Rapoport, R.   85, 86
Rapoport, R.N.   85, 86
Reid, G.L.   207
Reid, W.H.   178
Ritzer, G.   50
Rogers, E.M.   17
Rosenthal, R.A.   49, 68, 132
Roth, J.   205, 209
Ruddock, R.   ii, 33

Sartre, J.P.   66
Sayles, L.R.   178
Schein, E.H.   150
Scott, W.R.   163
Seglow, P.   207
Shawe, R.W.   163
Shoemaker, F.F.   17
Simon, H.A.   132

Slater, P.E.   114
Snoek, J.D.   49, 68, 132
Sofer, C.   150
Speck, W.A.   177
Stephenson, R.M.   163
Strauss, A.   180, 188

Thomas, B.   207
Toffler, A.   27, 33,
Trice, H.M.   50
Trist, E.L.   132
Turner, G.   178

Vamplew, C.   150
Vroom, V.H.   90, 101

Ward, J.P.   208
Warmington, A.   xii, xiii, 4, 10, 11
Weber, M.   50
Wedderburn, D.   191, 207
Weir, D.   xiii, 3, 4, 13, 178
Whittaker, E.   181, 189
Wickens, J.D.   163
Willmott, P.   17, 85
Wolfe, D.M.   49, 68, 86, 132
Wood, S.   xiii, 3, 4, 14
Worsley, P.   178

Yalom, I.D.   208
Yerkes, R.M.   27, 33
Yetton, P.W.   xiii, xiv, 4, 9, 16, 90, 101
Young, M.   17, 85

See also the Bibliography

SUBJECT INDEX

Abkhasians 15
Absenteeism 46, 128
Accountability 45, 53
Accounting Mechanisms 185-6
Achievement 6, 7, 16
- Inability to 41-2, 43
- Need for 7, 195, 203
- Orientation 111, 194, 196

Adolescence 185, 186
Alienation 9, 107-9, 203, 204
Analysis Levels of 3
- Culture 3, 11
- Group 3
- Individual 3
- Organization 3, 11

Anxiety passim
  Definitions of 36-7
Authority - see Power

'Backbone Managers' 199
'Beating The System' 171-2
Bureaucracy, 61, 64, 105-7, 109, 137, 140, 143, 182
- Reactions to 106, 109-10
- 'Death of' 106
  See also Hierarchy

Capital
- Return on 40

Capitalism
- Ills of 204

Career 8, 60, 72-85, 135, 180-8, 199, 204, 206
- Blockages to 201
- History 124
- Patterns 141
- Uncertainties 10, 135, 140-1
  See also 'Dual-Career Families'

Change 6, 15, 113, 115-31, 133-49, 182, 205
- Facilitation of 124, 130
- Management of 134-49

    - Resistance to   123-7, 134-5, 201
  See also Innovation
Change Agent   134-49
Change Programme   133-49
    Acceptability of   134, 140, 143-4, 145
Commitment   72-3, 104, 112, 146, 186, 206
Communication   129, 134, 136, 147
Community   57, 59, 61, 65, 77
Conflict   7, 9, 10, 13, 15, 16, 35, 90-100, 112, 113, 123-7, 135, 142-4, 159-62
    Avoidance of   9, 99-100
  See also Role Conflict
Consultation   129, 147
Contingency   9, 109, 113-14, 180, 182, 188
  See Leadership, Models
Control   6, 10, 15, 120, 166
    - Systems of   39-40, 57, 137, 144, 157
    - Unilateral   64
  See also Overcontrol, Undercontrol
Cosmopolitans   60
Costs   108
    Reduction of   39
Counselling   198
Crime   170
'Cross of Relationships'   54-64
  See also Role Set
Culture   14, 42
    - Organizational   57
    - Change   146, 149
  See also Management Values, Subterranean Values, Values

Decision Making   9, 89-100, 102-14, 115-31, 134, 142, 143-4, 149, 175
Defence Mechanisms   5, 16, 28, 30
Delegation   5, 6, 32, 58, 103-114
Delivery Dates   108
Deprivation   9, 111-12, 114
Development Activities   147
Deviance   13, 108, 170, 172, 198
  See also Secondary Deviation
Dissonance, Reduction of   145-9

'Discovery Syndrome'   175-6
'Dual Career Families'   80-5
'Dynamic Tension'   16

Effort   42-3, 111
  See also Reward
Ends   35, 44-5, 47-9
  See also Means
Enterpreneurship   175, 195, 203
Environment   61-2, 110, 118-19, 128, 133-4
Expectations   14, 66, 141-2, 155, 162, 182, 196
      - Settled   197

Failure   42, 53, 65, 127, 182, 187, 197, 198, 199,
      201, 202, 203
Families   8, 70-85
  See also 'Dual Career Families'
        Joint Conjugal Role Relationships
        Segregated Conjugal Role Relationships
Feedback   128
Flexibility   15, 147, 196, 201
'Four Task Model'   54, 62-4
Frames of Reference
      - Changed   136
      - Psychological   3
      - Social Psychological 3
      - Sociological   3
Functional Interdependence   155

Goal Congruence   90-100
Goals   40
      - Displacement of   146
Group Work   198
Growth   40, 57, 63-4

'Hidden Contract'   72-80, 83-5
Hierarchy   15, 104-7, 111, 121, 125, 137, 139, 143,
      195, 203, 204, 206
  See also Bureaucracy

Identity   14, 73, 77-9, 82, 184
      - Stress   179-81, 185-8
  See also Self-esteem
Ideology   14, 198-206
Ignorance   129, 173-4
Induction, Problems of   138-9, 145
Industrial Relations   39, 40, 159-60
Information   126, 128-9, 174
  See also 'Misinformation'
Innovation   9, 15, 115-31, 133-49, 160
      - Computer   10, 115-31
      - 'Conformist'   47
      - 'Deviant'   48
  See also Change

Job Enlargement   175
Job Enrichment   32
Job Satisfaction   104, 158
Job Security   123, 125, 199, 202, 204, 206
Joint Conjugal Role Relationships   71-85
'Joking Relationships'   181

Knowledge   115, 117, 120-22, 126-8, 131, 143
      - Principle of Minimum   173

Labels   14, 201
Labour Market   191, 198, 202
Labour Mobility   73, 190, 199-200, 203, 204, 206
Labour Turnover   122-3, 128, 165
Leadership   9, 89-100
      - Contigency Models of   9, 90, 94
      - Traditional Models of   94
Learning   5, 27, 28, 30-1, 64, 130
Legitimacy   6, 35, 43-9
      - of Authority   43-9
      - of Change Programmes   134, 138, 140, 143-4, 147-8
      - of New Role Relationships   10, 121
  See also Power
Love   64
'Luck Labelling'   14, 181, 185-8

Management
- by Exception   57
- by Objectives   40-1, 57, 158
- Prerogatives   102-14
- Style   6, 62, 89-100, 134, 144
- Values   128
  See also Values
'Managerial Problems'   2
Managers   passim
- for Managers in General, see especially Chapter 3
- for Computer Specialists, see especially Chapter 7
- for Internal Consultants/Change Agents, see especially Chapter 8
- for Personnel Managers, see especially Chapter 2
Manipulation   158-9
Marriage   70-86
  See also Families
Matrix Organization   110
Means   35, 44-5, 47-9
  See also Ends
Mental Instability   187
Meritocracy   196, 197, 203
'Misinformation'   174-5
Mismatch   7, 8, 14, 15, 35, 42, 49, 51, 62, 105, 112
Modelling   2-5, 53, 64
  See also Leadership, Models
Models
- Contingency   9, 90, 94
- Descriptive   89
- Mathematical   174
- Normative   98-100
- Traditional   94
  See also Contingency, Leadership
Monitoring   128-9, 175
Motivation   25, 27

New Broom   176
'Normal' Individual   194-5

Obligations   72-85, 155, 158
'Old Soldiering'   177

231

Organization   passim
- Chart   55, 57
- Design   107, 162, 205
- Development   62
  See also Change, Innovation, Matrix Organization, Performance
Over Control   13, 15, 168-77
Overload   42, 43
Outcomes   23-4
- Uncertainty of   23, 27, 39
- Importance of   24, 27, 53
- Ability to Influence 24, 28

Participation   9, 58, 89-100, 102-14
Pension Schemes   204-5
Performance   6, 9, 15
- Individual   27, 35, 58, 107-9, 159, 162, 200
- Organizational   105-7, 109, 134, 148, 162
  See also Success, Success Criteria
Performance Appraisal   39, 40-2, 135, 137, 187
  See also Success, Success Criteria
Pilfering   166, 168, 177
Politics   10, 52
- of Innovation   118, 125-7, 129-30
- Organizational   41, 129
Power   15-16, 123-4, 135
- Actual   104-7
- Formal   104-7
- Legitimate 105, 137
Prerogatives
  See Management
Process   12, 13, 153, 159, 160, 163, 182
- Definitions of   157
Productivity   39, 108
Professionalization   48, 61, 64, 196, 199, 205
Profits   39, 108
Profit Centre Management   57-8
Project Management   58, 110
Promotion   14, 39, 42, 73, 76, 137, 158, 182-3, 197
  See also Career
Protestant (Work) Ethic   188, 203

232

Psychologism   204

Quality   39-40, 108

Raw Materials   184
Rebellion   48
Rectification, Systems of   128
Redundancy   14, 122, 190-206
- Economic Effects of   190-1
- Inevitability of   200-6
- Management Development
  Solution to   199-200
- Psychological Effects of   191-2
- and Rationality   200
- Social Significance of   192

  See also Labour Market, Labour Mobility, Resilience
Relationships
- Intergroup   92-100, 134-49
- Interpersonal   92-100, 107-9
- with Peers   54, 58-9
- with Subordinates   54, 57-8
- with Superiors   54, 56-7
- with 'Users and
  Opposite Numbers'   54, 59-61
  Multiplicative   24-5
Resilience   193, 195, 196, 197, 198, 201
Responsibility, Allocation of   130, 195
Resources
- Allocation of   126-7
- Scarcity of   126-7

Retreatism   48
Rewards   16, 39, 42, 111
- Legitimation of   195

  See also Achievement, Career, Promotion
Risk   9, 10, 14, 117-19, 141-3
  See also Uncertainty
Role   6, 38-40, 119-22
- Ambiguity   39, 43, 107-9
- Change   117, 135-6, 139-40
- Conflict   8, 16, 35, 38-39, 77-80,
             82-3, 104-112, 139-40, 144

        - Differentiation   150
        - Strain   130
        - Uncertainty   130
  See also Change, Conflict, Legitimacy, Uncertainty
Role Set 6, 38
Roles, General
        - Active   10, 119
        - Arbitrator   160
        - Communicator   122
        - Consumer   71-85
        - Diagnostician   122
        - Integrator   57
        - Passive   10, 120
        - Productive   71-85
        - Outsider   10, 136-40
        - Specialist   16, 43-6
Roles, Managerial
  See Managers
Routinization 47, 135
Rules 155, 169-77

Sanctions 39, 155, 158
  See also Rewards
Scapegoating 172
Secondary Deviation 170
  See also Deviance
Segregated Conjugal Role Relationships 71-85
Self-esteem 42
  See also Identity
'Shot in The Dark' 176
Skill 23, 64-5, 98-9, 122, 126, 131, 143
Socialization 9, 136, 180
        - Primary   99-100
        - Professional   181
Specialization 56, 62, 64, 73
Status 47-8, 77, 79, 111, 118, 125, 127, 135, 137,
      139, 196
Stock 166-77
        - Buffer   169, 177
        - Deficit   166
Stress passim
        - Activation of   5, 23, 25-7, 32

- Adaption Perspective 8
- Aphorisms on Managing 67-8
- Avoidance of 5, 6, 7, 13, 16, 28-9, 112, 121, 128, 160-2
- Coping with 28-31, 46-49, 64-67, 113-14, 127-31, 145-8, 185-9
- Definitions of 5, 9, 13, 16, 21-7, 36-42, 75, 90, 154, 167-8 192-4
- Elimination of 192, 198-206
- Experimental Evidence 37, 208
- Functions of 131, 162
- the Individual passim
- 'Labelling Perspective 11, 14
- Organizational 157-162, 167-8
- Physical Effects of 22, 52, 154
- 'Power-Conflict Perspective' 9
- Psychological Effects of 22, 52, 154
- 'Structural Perspective 11
- Transfer of 13, 16, 157-62

Strikes 46, 128
Structure 12, 13, 134, 137-8, 153, 154, 159, 160, 163
- Definitions of 12, 154-7
- Social 12, 137, 154-7
  See also Hierarchy
Subterranean Values 203
  See also Management Values, Values
Success 203, 204, 206
- Criteria 6, 11, 16, 35, 39-43, 135, 137, 142-3, 146, 182

Tasks
- Nature of 184
- Uncertainty in 141-3
Tedium 31-2

T-Groups   195, 196, 202
Theoretical Constructs   2
Time Dimensions   136, 186-7
Training   122-147
Troubleshooting   63

Uncertainty   6, 7, 9, 10, 14, 53, 115-31, 133-49,
         183-4
   See also Outcomes, Risks
Undercontrol   15

Values   65, 135, 180
   See also Culture, Management Values
            Subterranean Values
Variety, Reduction of   2
Vocabularies of Motive   201

Welfare Corporatism   206
Widget Systems   165-78